Accounting for Software

Accounting for Software

Robert McGee
CMA, CPA, CIA, CBA

DOW JONES-IRWIN
Homewood, Illinois 60430

```
HF 5681 .C57 M37 1985 c.1
McGee, Robert W.
Accounting for software
```

© DOW JONES-IRWIN, 1985

All rights reserved. No part of this publication may be reproduced, stored in a retrieval system, or transmitted, in any form or by any means, electronic, mechanical, photocopying, recording, or otherwise, without the prior written permission of the publisher.

This publication is designed to provide accurate and authoritative information in regard to the subject matter covered. It is sold with the understanding that the publisher is not engaged in rendering legal, accounting, or other professional service. If legal advice or other expert assistance is required, the services of a competent professional person should be sought.

From a Declaration of Principles jointly adopted by a Committee of the American Bar Association and a Committee of Publishers.

ISBN 0-87094-468-1
Library of Congress Catalog Card No. 83-73712

Printed in the United States of America

1 2 3 4 5 6 7 8 9 0 K 2 1 0 9 8 7 6 5

Preface

Prior to June 1969, accounting for software did not present a problem. Software was purchased in conjunction with hardware, and the purchase price did not separately state the portion that was attributable to software, so software was accounted for as part of the hardware. In June 1969, IBM, the largest seller of computer hardware, began to separately state the prices charged for its hardware and software. This change in policy by IBM was soon followed by changes in the way other hardware manufacturers accounted for software sales. As a result of this change in billing practice, companies that purchased software were able to comparison-shop for the first time. It was no longer necessary to purchase hardware and software from the same seller.

The result of this policy change led to the development of a new industry, the software industry. Companies that never manufactured computer hardware began making and selling a wide variety of software products. Entry into this new industry was fairly easy. Initial investment was small. A programmer with an entrepreneurial bent could start developing software part-time in the basement or spare room at home. In fact, many of the more than 4,000 companies presently producing software in the United States started in this manner.

As companies began to purchase software from these firms, it became necessary to decide whether the software should be amortized over the same period as the related hardware, or whether some other period should be used instead. The problem of accounting for software costs became more complex when companies began to develop their own software for internal use. Prior to IBM's "unbundling" in June 1969, it was not necessary for a company to develop its own software, because the software could be obtained at no cost from the hardware manufacturers. As software began to be constructed for internal use it became necessary to decide whether the costs of constructing this software should be charged to expense as incurred or capitalized and amortized over the expected period of benefit.

This book came about as a result of the many inquiries received on this topic by the National Association of Accountants. Upon investigation, it became clear that the existing literature did not provide the needed guidance, and this book was written to provide that guidance. Several surveys were conducted to determine current practices for both software vendor companies and software users. The accounting policies for both purchased and constructed software were examined.

This book provides guidance to accountants who need to formulate a policy of accounting for software. The issues relating to purchased and constructed software are examined from both the software vendor and user perspectives. This book provides a comprehensive analysis of the major issues related to accounting for software.

Robert McGee

Acknowledgments

As is true of any research project, there are many more people involved in bringing the project to a successful conclusion than just the author. This project is no exception. I am grateful to the National Association of Accountants, which partially funded this project. I also owe a debt to the people who granted me interviews, and to the NAA's Management Accounting Practices Committee and Subcommittee on MAP Statement Promulgation, whose members reviewed my questionnaires and made many valuable suggestions, as did the members of AICPA's task force on software accounting. I am also indebted to the review panel members who volunteered many good suggestions, and to the executives who took time from their busy schedules to complete the questionnaires.

The Seton Hall University research department, headed by Dr. Helena Wisniewski, and Christopher Held, my research associate, deserve recognition for the assistance they provided in assembling the mailing lists and questionnaire responses. Thanks also go to Robert Kueppers of Deloitte Haskins & Sells in New York, who gave me access to their NAARS subscription, and to Louis Bisgay, Alfred M. King and Robert L. Shultis of the National Association of Accountants, who gave me the freedom to conduct the research as I saw fit. A special thanks goes to Miriam Redrick, NAA librarian, who assisted in the literature search, and to the people in NAA's word processing center who typed the manuscript.

Portions of this research were used to partially fulfill the doctoral degree requirements at the University of Warwick, Coventry, England, under the supervision of Professor R. A. Fawthrop. Any errors or weaknesses in this treatise are attributable to the author alone.

R. M.

Contents

1. **Financial Accounting for Software**   1

    Background: *The Beginning of the Problem—How to Account for Software. What Is Software? The Tangibility Issue. Financial Accounting Rules.* Deficiencies in Current Pronouncements: *FASB Statement No. 2. FASB Interpretation No. 6. Technical Bulletin No. 79-2.* Related Pronouncements: *The Record and Music Industry. Motion Picture Films. Research and Development Arrangements.* Software Costs: Should They Be Capitalized or Expensed? *The Controversy. The Catalyst.* Author's Views.

2. **Software Vendor Revenue and Cost Recognition Policies for Software**   18

    Introduction.

3. **Survey of Software Vendors**   53

    Introduction.

4. **Software-User Accounting Policies and Practices**   64

    Introduction.

5. **Survey of Software Users**   78

    Introduction.

6. **The Effects of Software Accounting Policy on Bank Lending Decisions**   88

    Background. The Present Study. Summary and Conclusions.

7.   **Taxation of Software**   **105**
     Background. What Is Software? Tangible versus Intangible.
     The Film Cases. Cases Involving the Sale of Information:
     *Stock Exchange Data. Credit Information. Mailing Lists.
     Artwork.* Cases Involving the Uniform Commercial Code.
     Cases Involving Data Processing Service Bureaus. Cases In-
     volving the Sale of Software. 1983—A Turning Point or an Ab-
     erration?

Notes to Chapters   **133**
Appendix A.   Methodology   **149**
Appendix B.   Internal Revenue Service Pronouncements on
                  Software   **153**
Appendix C.   Sales and Use Tax Status of Software by State   **158**
Bibliography   **161**
Index   **167**

CHAPTER 1

Financial Accounting for Software

Background

In the decade following World War II, companies began to use computers to solve business problems and process data to an ever-increasing extent. At this early stage in the development of the computer industry, the companies that manufactured computer hardware also produced the software that was used with the machines. These manufacturers generally sold the systems software as part of the hardware without breaking down the purchase price into its hardware and software components. The companies that used the hardware hired employees to construct whatever "custom" software that might be needed. Very few companies constructed systems or applications software for sale apart from sales that were "bundled" with hardware.

As the use of computers became more prevalent in the 1960s, the demand for custom programming increased and led to the development of a new industry that would supply these software users with the programs they needed. However, it was still not a common practice to purchase application programs, because these were supplied free of charge by the hardware manufacturer.

In June 1969, the policy of bundling hardware and software costs changed when the International Business Machines Corporation (IBM) decided to "unbundle"—that is, to state the cost of the software and hardware separately.[1] This policy resulted in the creation of a new industry, the software industry, whose members began to produce software for sale to users of hardware. Companies that formerly wrote their own software now had an option—they could purchase it. This option became very attractive, as the cost of developing a program might run into six or seven figures, whereas a comparable program could be purchased for $50,000 or less. This cost relationship led to a rapid increase in the number of firms that manufacture software for sale, as a program that might cost $1 million to construct could be sold to a multitude of customers for $50,000 each. A software firm would be able to break even after only 20 sales. Any additional sales would be almost pure profit, as the cost of delivering a program is basically equal to the cost of the medium used (tape, disk, and so forth) plus selling expenses.

The Beginning of the Problem—How to Account for Software

In the same year IBM decided to unbundle, the Internal Revenue Service (IRS) issued a pronouncement addressing the software issue.[2] This Revenue Procedure provided tax accounting guidelines in connection with costs incurred to develop, purchase, or lease computer software. Basically, this procedure stated that the costs associated with the development of software could either be expensed as incurred or capitalized and amortized over five years or less. Thus, software development costs were to be accorded the same treatment as research and development costs for federal tax purposes.[3]

Purchased software could be capitalized along with the hardware if bundled. Software having a separately stated price could be amortized if treated as an intangible asset. Leased software is accorded the same treatment as rentals under regulation 1.162–11.

Two years after that pronouncement was issued, the IRS issued a second pronouncement dealing with software.[4] That ruling held that for depreciation and investment tax-credit purposes, the cost of a new computer includes software costs not separately stated and capitalized in accordance with the taxpayer's consistent practice. Another pronouncement, issued that same year, held that the capitalization of software costs with respect to a new computer where such costs had previously been expensed is a change in method of accounting requiring the commissioner's consent.[5]

What Is Software?

Prior to June 1969, when IBM unbundled and created the software industry, there was no need to define software for accounting purposes, because it was accounted for as part of the hardware. The few programs that were developed internally constituted such a small percentage of total expenditures for most companies that a formal software accounting policy was not needed.

However, as software expenditures continued to increase and become more material, companies began establishing specific policies for software accounting. It was then that the definition of software became important. Unfortunately, there is no single readily accepted definition of software. The broadest definition would be that software includes everything that is not hardware.[6] The definition of software promulgated by the National Bureau of Standards[7] and adopted by the U.S. Bureau of Standards[8] is: "Computer programs, procedures, rules, and possibly associated documentation concerned with the operation of a data processing system."

The IRS defines computer software as:

> all programs or routines used to cause a computer to perform a desired task or set of tasks, and the documentation required to describe and maintain those programs. Computer programs of all classes, for example, operating systems, executive systems, monitors, compilers and translators, assembly routines, and utility programs as well as application programs are included. 'Computer software' does not include procedures which are external to computer operations, such as instructions to transcription operators and external control procedures.[9]

Several courts and state legislatures have also defined software. Some have even made distinctions between systems software and applications software. The Supreme Court of Tennessee has defined a systems (operational) program as one that is fundamental to the functioning of the hardware, or software that controls the hardware and makes it run.[10]

Bryant and Mather state that systems software consists of:

1. Compilers, which are used to translate symbolic code into machine language, and which are also capable of replacing a series of instructions with subroutines.
2. Sorts, which assemble and file items of data in a certain sequence or order.
3. Utility routines, which perform functions such as transferring data from one magnetic tape to another.[11]

The Tangibility Issue

Another problem that grew out of unbundling is the issue of tangibility. The IRS treats software as intangible and, therefore, not eligible for the investment tax credit unless bundled with hardware,[12] but at least one court has ruled that software is tangible and qualifies for the investment tax credit.[13] For state sales,[14] use,[15] and property[16] tax purposes, the majority of courts have held that software is intangible and therefore, not subject to the tax. However, two recent cases have held otherwise.[17] For Uniform Commercial Code (UCC)[18] and replevin[19] purposes, software is tangible, but nor for collapsible corporation purposes.[20] The sale of a prewritten program is currently taxable in 33 states and exempt in 13, with a few states not yet taking a position one way or the other.

Financial Accounting Rules

The present financial accounting rules pertaining to computer software are far from clear. The Financial Accounting Standards Board (FASB) has issued several pronouncements that deal with software to a limited extent. One pronouncement requires that research and development costs must be expensed as incurred, unless an alternative future use exists.[21] Another pronouncement states that not all software costs are to be considered research and development costs.[22] A third pronouncement asserts that software costs not qualifying as research and development expenditures are not necessarily inventoriable or deferrable.[23] None of the FASB pronouncements give clear guidance regarding when computer software qualifies for capitalization treatment, and whether the software costs should be included in the balance sheet as tangible or intangible assets, although *FASB Interpretation No. 6*, par. 8, footnote 2, seems to indicate that software should be classified as intangible.[24]

The Accounting Principles Board (APB), the predecessor of FASB, issued a pronouncement requiring intangibles acquired from others to be recorded as assets and amortized using the straight-line method, unless some other method was more appropriate.[25] The opinion went on to state that the cost of developing intangibles that are not specifically identifiable should be expensed as incurred. The issue of how to account for identifiable internally developed intangibles is not addressed, and it is questionable whether computer software should be classified as intangible in any event, since the courts seem unable to agree on the tangibility of software.

Deficiencies in Current Pronouncements

FASB Statement No. 2

FASB's statement on research and development provides as much ambiguity as it does guidance.[26] Paragraph 8 (*a*) defines research as:

> planned search or critical investigation aimed at discovery of new knowledge with the hope that such knowledge will be useful in developing a new product or service or a new process or technique or in bringing about a significant improvement to an existing product or process.

Research is an activity that occurs early in the software construction process, and although *FASB Statement No. 2* requires that research expenditures be charged to expense as incurred, there is little guidance regarding which activities should be classified as research.

Paragraph 8 (*b*) defines development as

> the translation of research findings or other knowledge into a plan or design for a new product or process or for a significant improvement to an existing

product or process whether intended for sale or use. It includes the conceptual formulation, design, and testing of product alternatives, construction of prototypes, and operation of pilot plants. It does not include routine or periodic alterations to existing products, production lines, manufacturing processes, and other ongoing operations even though those alterations may represent improvements, and it does not include market research or market testing activities.

This definition of development can be applied to software accounting in two different ways. It could be interpreted to mean that the development phase does not end until software construction is essentially complete because successful completion is uncertain until the development process is nearly complete. For the development phase to end, it is necessary to have a working prototype. Lastly, the fact that design modifications are needed throughout the construction phase is evidence that development occurs through that phase.

Another interpretation could be that the development phase has essentially been completed before the construction phase begins, and any design modifications that occur during construction are minor in nature and are not part of the development phase. The formulation, design, and product-testing activities occur prior to the construction phase. In fact, there must be a single-product design before construction can commence, and although testing occurs during the construction phase, the testing at that stage involves the product's operation rather than the testing of alternative products. Futhermore, the software construction process does not culminate in the production of a prototype or the operation of a pilot plant, so these guidelines are irrelevant for purposes of determining when the development phase ends and the production phase begins. The key point for determining when development has ended should be the establishment of technological feasibility instead.

Paragraph 31 states:

Computer software is developed for many and diverse uses. Accordingly, in each case the nature of the activity for which the software is being developed should be considered in relation to the guidelines in paragraphs 8–10 to determine whether software costs should be included or excluded. For example, efforts to develop a new or higher level of computer software capability intended for sale (but not under a contractual arrangement) would be a research and development activity.

The phrase "new or higher level of computer software capability" can be interpreted in several ways. If "new" is interpreted in the technological sense, most software would be excluded, as most software is developed using existing rather than new technology. "New" could also refer to whether the product is new in the company sense, even though developed with existing technology. "New" could also be interpreted to mean new in the market sense. For example, the first company to develop and market a payroll program incurs development costs, but companies that later on develop a similar product do not incur development costs.

The phrase "efforts to develop" could also be interpreted to include the whole construction process, which would place all construction expenditures in the development phase. Or, it could be interpreted to mean that "efforts to develop" cease prior to the construction phase. These two interpretations lead to opposite results, as construction expenditures would be classified as development costs calling for expense treatment in the first instance, and such expenditures would be nonresearch and development costs in the second instance and might call for capitalization treatment instead.

Paragraph 9 of *FASB Statement No. 2* provides several examples of activities that could be considered research and development expenditures. These are:

(*a*) Laboratory research aimed at discovery of new knowledge.
(*b*) Searching for applications of new research findings or other knowledge.
(*c*) Conceptual formulation and design of possible product or process alternatives.
(*d*) Testing in search for or evaluation of product or process alternatives.
(*e*) Modification of the formulation or design of a product or process.
(*f*) Design, construction, and testing of preproduction prototypes and models.
(*g*) Design of tools, jigs, molds, and dies involving new technology.
(*h*) Design, construction, and operation of a pilot plant that is not of a scale economically feasible to the enterprise for commercial production.
(*i*) Engineering activity required to advance the design of a product to the point that it meets specific functional and economic requirements and is ready for manufacture.

The first four activities generally occur prior to the construction phase. The fifth example, "modification of the formulation or design of a product or process," can occur throughout the process but occurs only to a minimal degree once the construction process begins. As was previously mentioned, design modifications can be viewed as either occurring as part of the development phase or as part of the construction phase after development is completed.

Examples (*f*) through (*h*) are viewed by some as not being applicable to software accounting. The end product is not a prototype but rather is the product itself. Others view the prototype as being the end product itself in the case of software, which would place the entire software construction process within the definition of research and development and, therefore, subject to expense treatment.

The last example relates to engineering activity. One view holds that manufacturing is merely the duplication of the program once the program is ready to market and that all activity occurring prior to this point is research and development. Others view all engineering activity as occurring prior to construction.

Paragraph 10 lists examples of activities that typically would be excluded from research and development. These activities include:

(*a*) Engineering follow-through in an early phase of commercial production.
(*b*) Quality control during commercial production including routine testing of products.
(*c*) Troubleshooting in connection with breakdowns during commercial production.
(*d*) Routine, ongoing efforts to refine, enrich, or otherwise improve upon the qualities of an existing product.
(*e*) Adaptation of an existing capability to a particular requirement or customer's need as part of a continuing commercial activity.
(*f*) Seasonal or other periodic design changes to existing products.
(*g*) Routine design of tools, jigs, molds, and dies.
(*h*) Activity, including design and construction engineering, related to the construction, relocation, rearrangement, or start-up of facilities or equipment other than (1) pilot plants . . . and (2) facilities or equipment whose sole use is for a particular research and development project. . . .
(*i*) Legal work in connection with patent applications or litigation, and the sale or licensing of patents.

The first three examples are subject to several interpretations. These activities could be viewed as occurring only after sales have commenced, and that similar activities that occur during construction are part of development. Another view is that these activities constitute construction and post-construction activities, which is a further indication that construction costs should not be considered part of development.

FASB INTERPRETATION NO. 6

Another FASB pronouncement states that:

> costs, including those incurred for programming and testing software, are research and development costs when incurred in the search for or the evaluation of product or process alternatives or in the design of a preproduction model.[27]

The phrase "search for or the evaluation of product or process alternatives" is subject to varying interpretations, as was previously mentioned, depending on whether development is regarded as being virtually complete at the beginning of construction or at the end. The phrase "preproduction model" is not defined, and its meaning is not clear as applied to software. The preproduction model could be interpreted to mean the same thing as a prototype, and all costs incurred prior to the completion of the prototype could be viewed as research and development costs. Another view is that preproduction models are not made for software, although systems make-ups or product simulators are sometimes made prior to construction.

This pronouncement also states that:

> costs for programming and testing are not research and development costs when incurred, for example, in routine or other ongoing efforts to improve an existing product or adapt a product to a particular requirement or customer's need.[28]

This statement could be interpreted to mean that programming and testing costs are not research and development expenditures only when they are incurred to improve an existing product or adapt a product to a particular requirement or customer's need. Or, it could be interpreted less restrictively to exclude programming and testing costs from classification as research and development for activities other than those given in the example. Furthermore, it could be argued that zeroing in on the costs associated with product improvement or adaptation misses the point entirely, and that the issue to be addressed should be accounting for construction costs. Lastly, one could conclude by a literal reading of the Interpretation that all enhancement costs should be classified as nonresearch and development. However, it could be argued that such a view is not reasonable. The process involved in producing enhancements to an existing product is essentially the same as that for a new product, and some of the costs involved in the construction of a new product are research and development costs.

Technical Bulletin No. 79-2

This pronouncement states that:

> all costs incurred in producing a given software product or process are not necessarily research and development costs. However, a determination that software production costs are not research and development costs does not necessarily mean that they would be inventoriable or deferrable to future operations. Those decisions can only be made in light of all of the facts and circumstances surrounding the particular situation.[29]

From reading this pronouncement one can quickly conclude that very little guidance, if any, is being provided. The issue of which costs should be classified as research and development is not addressed. Although there is a hint that certain costs may be deferrable or inventoriable under certain circumstances, there is no suggestion elaborating on when such circumstances might arise.

Related Pronouncements

The Record and Music Industry

The argument can be made that the cost of producing a record master is similar to the cost of producing a computer program. In both cases:

1. The majority of the product's value is the result of the labor that is expended rather than the matierial that is used.
2. Logical patterns must be developed (coding or music, either in written or nonwritten form) and transferred onto a physical medium such as a record, tape, or disk (although this is not necessarily the case for a computer program, which may be input directly into the computer).
3. The value of the finished product far exceeds the value of the material upon which the coding or music is recorded.
4. Both records and computer programs developed for sale have estimated economic lives and projected income streams that are difficult, but not impossible, to predict.

The National Commission on New Technological Uses of Copyrighted Works stated that:

> Both recorded music and computer programs are sets of information in a form which, when passed over a magnetized head, cause minute currents to flow in such a way that desired physical work is accomplished.[30]

On the other hand, it can also be argued that records are of a different nature than computer programs that are recorded on disks or tapes.[31] For example, when information is transferred from a tape into the computer, the tape is no longer of any value to the user. In many cases, the tape is not even retained by the user. It may be discarded or returned. The information on the tape, unlike a phonograph record, is not complete and ready to be used at the time of its purchase. It must be translated into a language that is understood by the computer.

Secondly, a computer tape or disk is not necessary to transmit information. Such information can also be sent over telephone wires or by satellite or may even be programmed directly by the originator of the program.

In late 1981, FASB issued a statement that permits the capitalization of a record master in instances where past performance and current popularity of the artist provides a sound basis for estimating that the cost will be recovered from future sales.

> The portion of the cost of a record master borne by the record company shall be reported as an asset if the past performance and current popularity of the artist provides a sound basis for estimating that the cost will be recovered from future sales. Otherwise, that cost shall be charged to expense. The amount recognized as an asset shall be amortized over the estimated life of the recorded

performance using a method that reasonably relates the amount to the net revenue expected to be realized.[32]

That same statement goes on to define record master as:

The master tape resulting from the performance of the artist. It is used to produce molds for commercial record production and other tapes for use in making cartridges, cassettes, and reel tapes. The costs of producing a record master include (a) the cost of the musical talent (musicians, vocal background, and arrangements); (b) the cost of the technical talent for engineering, directing, and mixing; (c) costs for the use of the equipment to record and produce the master; and, (d) studio facility charges.[33]

In its comment letter to the Exposure Draft that eventually became *Statement No. 50,* Coopers & Lybrand suggested that the language of the statement be changed to specifically include music publishers.[34] Similar suggestions were made by other respondents,[35] and to also include record producers and songwriters.[36]

Motion Picture Films

Another statement that might be related to computer software costs is *FASB Statement No. 53,* "Financial Reporting by Producers and Distributors of Motion Picture Films," which allows the capitalization of film-production costs.[37] This statement requires that film-production costs be capitalized as film cost inventory and be amortized using the individual-film-forecast-computation method[38] or the periodic-table-computation method.[39] The individual-film-forecast-computation method amortizes costs in the ratio of current gross revenues to anticipated total gross revenues, with adjustment for periodic changes in estimate.[40] The periodic-table-computation method amortizes film costs using the historic revenue patterns of a large group of films.[41]

The analogy of motion picture films to software has also been made in several court cases, and several court cases dealing with sales, use, property, and federal taxation of motion picture films or master negatives have been cited by courts hearing software tax issues.[42]

Research and Development Arrangements

Another FASB statement addresses the topic of research and development arrangements.[43] During the course of several interviews conducted as part of this research project, it was pointed out that some software vending companies enter into research and development arrangements so that they can treat costs that would otherwise be expensed as assets instead. These arrangements may be structured so that a separate entity undertakes the task of constructing software that would otherwise be constructed internally and then sells the finished software product to the arranging firm, which then promptly records the software as an asset. Had the software been constructed internally instead, there would be pressure to expense the construction cost as research and development. The survey that was mailed to software vendors bore this theory out to a limited extent, although the responses revealed that a very small percentage of software vendors participate in research and development arrangements, and those that do have valid business reasons for doing so apart from the beneficial financial statement effect.[44]

Software Costs: Should They Be Capitalized or Expensed?

Prior to June 1969, when IBM unbundled, this question was not an issue. Software costs were included in the price of the hardware and were amortized over the useful life of the hardware. After IBM began stating their software prices separately from their hardware prices, and as firms began to develop their own software, this quesiton began to be raised with increasing frequency. Over the past two decades, software costs have become an increasingly important expenditure in most corporate budgets. While it was easy to expense relatively minor software costs in the past, for reasons of materiality, it has become increasingly difficult to state emphatically that software expenditures are immaterial when they continue to increase every year.[45]

FASB Concepts Statement No. 3 defines assets as:

> probable future economic benefits obtained or controlled by a particular entity as a result of past transactions or events.

The statement goes on to say that:

> An asset has three essential characteristics: (*a*) it embodies a probable future benefit that involves a capacity, singly or in combination with other assets, to contribute directly or indirectly to future net cash inflows, (*b*) a particular enterprise can obtain the benefit and control others' access to it, and (*c*) the transaction or other event giving rise to the enterprise's right to or control of the benefit has already occurred.

Expenses, on the other hand, have doubtful future economic benefit. From these criteria, the answer seems simple. Software that has probable future economic benefit should be recorded as an asset and amortized over its estimated economic life. Software having doubtful future economic benefit should be expensed. Unfortunately, the answer is not quite that simple. Some accountants argue for capitalization,[46] while others continue to argue for expense treatment.[47] Several articles have addressed the topic in recent years, and it appears that the issue will continue to be in the news for the next few years.[48] The American Institute of Certified Public Accountants (AICPA) has formed a task force to study the issue,[49] and the Securities and Exchange Commission (SEC) has imposed a moratorium on the capitalization of certain software costs.[50]

The Controversy

The controversy, simply stated, is deciding whether software costs should be classified as assets or expenses. However, the quesiton is more than just philosophical. The choice chosen can affect a company's earnings and its ability to raise capital. There are at least 4,000 companies in the United States that construct software for sale. For all of these companies, software expenditures are a significant percentage of net income, and choosing to classify software expenditures as assets or expenses can make the difference between making a profit or incurring a loss. One public company that reported a profit of $2.2 million in 1981 would have had a loss of $1 million that year if certain software expenditures had been expensed instead of capitalized. In 1982, the reported $2.5 million profit would have been a $4 million loss.[51] There is some evidence to suggest that accounting policy can affect expansion[52] and the ability to raise capital.[53] The interviews conducted in the course of this study and the questionnaire responses confirm this feeling.

The Catalyst

If there is one single event which caused the software accounting issue to come to life, it was the issuance by the Association of Data Processing Service Organizations (ADAPSO) of its Exposure Draft on software accounting in April 1982.[54] This Exposure Draft set down clear guidelines for accounting for software costs and revenues. Its issuance caused the AICPA to form a task force to study the issue.

Author's Views

1. Most software that is purchased or internally constructed does not fit the definition of research and development. Most software is constructed from existing technology using existing coding methods, and any research and development that occurs is at the early stages prior to construction. Software is beyond the development stage when technological feasibility is established.

The interviews conducted in conjunction with this study and the questionnaire survey results indicate that many companies automatically assume that internally constructed software falls within the definition of research and development and is, therefore, expensed. In the author's opinion, this view is incorrect. Each software project should be evaluated on its own merits and classified accordingly.

2. The accounting treatment for purchased software should be the same as that for comparable internally constructed software. If a company plans to use a payroll program or accounts receivable program for the next five years, the cost of obtaining that program should be amortized over five years, regardless of whether the software was purchased or internally constructed.

The interviews and questionnaire responses indicate that present practice for most companies calls for the expensing of internally constructed software and the capitalization of purchased software. The usual reasons for this practice are either that it is easier to determine the cost of purchased software or that a purchased software product has a better chance of having future economic benefit, because it has already been extensively tested and debugged. In the author's opinion, these reasons are not sufficient. Just because the cost of a purchased program is easier to determine is not sufficient reason to expense the costs of internally constructing comparable software. And once a project's feasibility has been determined, the risk of failure is small enough to warrant capitalization treatment. Furthermore, the production costs of motion picture films and records are already being capitalized, and the production process for software is similar in many ways to that for records and films.

3. The cost of internally constructed software can be broken down into the following six categories:

    a. Feasibility costs, and other costs incurred prior to design costs in the software product life cycle.
    b. Design costs.
    c. Coding costs.
    d. Testing costs.
    e. Support costs.
    f. Service costs.

In cases where the finished software product is expected to have future economic benefit, the costs that are incurred for designing, coding, and testing should be capitalized and amortized over the expected period of benefit. Predesign costs, such as feasibility costs, should be expensed, as should service and support costs, as these costs have doubtful future economic benefit and more nearly resemble period costs than capitalizable costs.

4. The straight-line method is an acceptable method of amortization for intangible assets. In cases where software is classified as intangible, this method can be used.

Accounting for Software

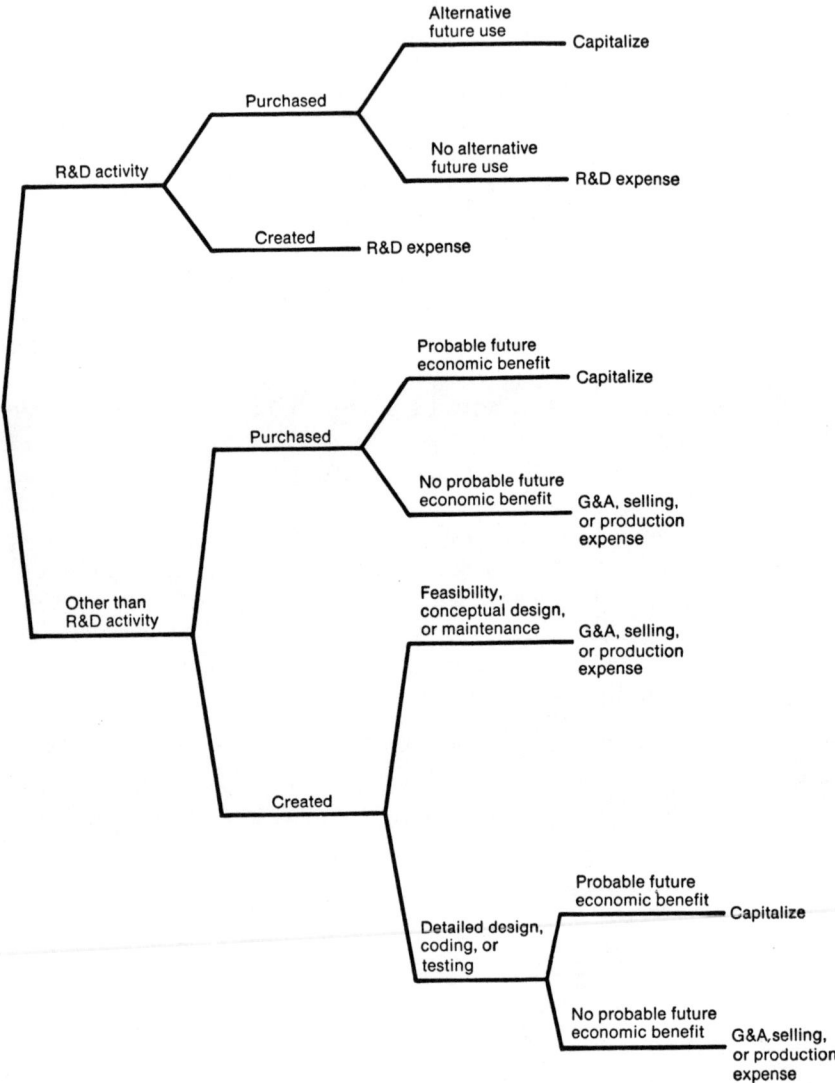

For software that is developed for sale, at least two other methods may also be considered. The period-table-computation method, which is sometimes used to amortize motion-picture-film costs, can also be used to amortize software intended for sale.

This method amortizes software costs prepared from historic revenue patterns of a large group of previously marketed software products. Although that revenue pattern is assumed to provide a reasonable guide to the experience of succeeding groups of software products produced and distributed under similar conditions, these tables should not be used for a software product that is expected to have a significantly different revenue pattern from those products which were included in the table. The periodic tables should be reviewed regularly and updated whenever revenue patterns change significantly.

Another acceptable method of amortization is the individual-software-forecast-computation method, a variation of which is used to amortize motion-picture-film production costs. This method may be illustrated by the following example:

Assume that a certain software product cost $18,000,000 to develop and is expected to generate revenues of $50,000,000 over its useful economic life. By the end of the second year, the amount of total anticipated revenues is reduced to $30,000,000 due to lagging sales. Actual revenue received in each of the first three years is:

First year	$10,000,000
Second year	6,000,000
Third year	5,000,000

Amortization in each of the first three years is computed as follows:

First year — *Amount of Amortization*

$$\frac{\$10,000,000}{\$50,000,000} \times \$18,000,000 = \underline{\$3,600,000}$$

Second Year

(a) Assuming change in anticipated total revenues from $50,000,000 to $30,000,000:

$$\frac{\$6,000,000}{\$20,000,000} \times \$14,400,000 = \underline{\$4,320,000}$$

Where:

(*1*) $6,000,000 is actual revenue in the second year;
(*2*) $20,000,000 is the adjusted total anticipated remaining revenue ($30,000,000 − $10,000,000); and
(*3*) $14,400,000 is original cost ($18,000,000) less accumulated amortization ($3,600,000).

(b) Assuming no change in anticipated total revenues:

$$\frac{\$6,000,000}{\$50,000,000} \times \$18,000,000 = \underline{\$2,160,000}$$

Third Year

(*a*) Assuming change in anticipated total revenues from $50,000,000 to $30,000,000:

$$\frac{\$5,000,000}{\$20,000,000} \times \$14,400,000 = \$3,600,000$$

The adjusted total anticipated remaining revenue ($20,000,000) and adjusted cost ($14,400,000) need not be reduced by the second year actual revenue ($6,000,000) and second year amortization ($4,320,000), respectively, because adjusted total anticipated remaining revenue ($20,000,000) did not change from the second to third year. If the reduction were made, the result would not change.

$$\frac{\$5,000,000}{\$20,000,000 - \$6,000,000} \times (\$14,400,000 - \$4,320,000) = \$3,600,000$$

(*b*) Assuming no change in anticipated total revenues:

$$\frac{\$5,000,000}{\$50,000,000} \times \$18,000,000 = \$1,800,000$$

Although the individual-software-forecast-computation method and the period-table-computation method may be appropriate amortization methods in certain instances, they are not necessarily the only acceptable methods. Other methods that reasonably relate the amount of the revenue expected to be realized to the amount of capitalized expenditures are also acceptable.

5. Software costs meeting the definition of research and development should be expensed as incurred in keeping with *FASB Statement No. 2*, unless the software has alternative future uses, in which case, it should be capitalized and amortized over the period of expected benefit. The alternative future use test does not apply to the internal development of computer software. See *FASB Interpretation No. 6*, par. 8, footnote 2.

6. Software expenditures classified as assets should be included in the "property, plant, and equipment" portion of the balance sheet if considered to be tangible property. Intangible software expenditures qualifying as assets should appear in the "other assets" section of the balance sheet.

7. Software expenditures should not be separately disclosed, unless they are material in amount. Software expenses can be considered material if they equal or exceed 5 percent of sales. Software assets can be considered material if they equal or exceed 5 percent of total assets. Disclosure may be by footnote or by separately stating software expenditures in the body of the income statement or balance sheet.

8. When the possibility exists to either acquire hardware and software "bundled" or "unbundled," the following factors should be considered:

a. *Amortization*—Software that might otherwise be expensed might be depreciated if combined with hardware costs. Likewise, software that would be capitalized if bundled might qualify for expense treatment if stated separately.

b. *Investment Tax Credit*—Software that would not otherwise qualify for the investment tax credit may so qualify if it is bundled with the related hardware. Even if software is acquired separately, the possibility of taking an investment tax credit should be examined. At least one court has held that the investment tax credit may be taken on unbundled software.

c. *Sales/Use Tax*—Bundling hardware and software may increase the amount of sales/use tax a buyer is required to pay. Some states do not tax the sale of software if sold separately from the hardware. Software delivered on cards, disk, or magnetic tape might be subject to tax in some states, even though the identical software, if delivered over telephone lines, would not be taxed.

d. *Property Tax*—Bundling hardware and software may increase the amount of property tax the owner must pay. Many states levy a property tax on tangible property only. Software is often classified as intangible property if accounted for separately from the hardware.

e. *Different Accounting Treatments*—The accounting treatment for financial reporting need not be the same as that used for tax reporting. Software expenditures may be expensed as incurred for tax purposes and capitalized and amortized for financial reporting purposes and vice versa. If different methods are used, the tax effect of the difference is reflected in the deferred tax account.

CHAPTER 2

Software Vendor Revenue and Cost Recognition Policies for Software

Introduction

This chapter is based on a survey of the accounting policies of 56 public companies in the computer software industry. The information has been organized in tabular form, with the companies listed alphabetically.

Some of the raw data used to construct this table was obtained with the assistance of Robert Kueppers of Deloitte Haskins & Sells in New York, who gave the author access to NAARS, a computer data base that is available by subscription from the American Institute of Certified Public Accountants (AICPA). Other data were obtained from annual reports, from 10-Ks and other Securities and Exchange Commission filings, and by telephone.

Survey of Accounting Policies—Public Companies in the Computer Software Industry

Company*	Type of Product	Revenue Recognition Policy	Accounting Policy for Cost of Developed or Acquired Software
1. AGS a. $65 million b. $33.8 million c. 12/31/82 d. Coopers & Lybrand	Systems development for service and high technology industries.	Service revenues rising from time and material contracts are recognized as services are rendered. Revenues from sales of software packages are recognized after substantial completion of the company's obligations under the terms of its contracts. Revenues from maintenance contracts are recognized ratably over the term of each contract. Product sales, costs of product sales, and related selling expenses are recorded when delivery is made to the customer.	Costs of software product enhancements with an established market are deferred and amortized over their estimated useful lives, generally five years.
2. AMS/REALSTAR, INC. a. $218 thousand b. $41 thousand c. 12/31/82 d. Arthur Andersen	Applications software for real estate industry.	Not disclosed.	Research and development costs are expensed as incurred and include programmers' direct salaries, software documentation costs, and other direct costs.
3. ADVANCED COMPUTER TECHNIQUES CORPORATION a. $18.4 million b. $5.7 million c. 12/31/82 d. Richard A. Eisner & Co.	Applications and systems software.	Information processing revenues are recognized in the period for which the service is provided. Software development revenues from time and materials contracts are recorded as services are performed. Revenues from fixed price software development contracts are recognized on the basis of estimated percentage of completion. Revisions in cost estimates and recognition of losses on these contracts are reflected in the	The cost of acquired software systems is being amortized on the straight-line method over five years. Development and enhancement costs, principally related to certain software packages, are charged to income when incurred. There was no charge to operations for such costs in the year ended December

*(a) annual revenues, (b) total assets, (c) end of fiscal year, and (d) auditor.

Survey of Accounting Policies (continued)

Company*	Type of Product	Revenue Recognition Policy	Accounting Policy for Cost of Developed or Acquired Software
		accounting period in which the facts become known. Contract terms provide for billing schedules that differ from revenue recognition and give rise to unbilled receivables and billings in excess of costs and profits. Revenue from software package license agreements is recognized upon delivery of the software. Under license agreements which require modification of the software package to the customer's specifications, revenue is recognized on the percentage of completion basis.	31, 1982, because all enhancements to existing products were funded by contracts with clients under which the company retained rights to the enhancements; amounts charged to operations for the years ended December 31, 1981, and 1980 were approximately $165,000 and $297,000, respectively.
4. AMERICAN SOFTWARE, INC. *a.* $16.1 million *b.* $25.7 million *c.* 4/30/83 *d.* Peat, Marwick, Mitchell & Co.	Applications software for IBM compatible computers.	Upon entering into a licensing agreement for proprietary software, the company recognizes 80 percent of the licensing fee upon delivery of the software documentation system and user manuals, 10 percent upon delivery of the computer tapes with source code, and 10 percent upon installation, conditioned upon at least 50 percent of the licensing fee being billable within 45 days, and installation contemplated within 180 days of execution of the licensing agreement. Otherwise, the company recognizes income on proprietary software as billed. Revenue related to custom programming, maintenance, and education is recognized as the related services are performed.	All costs associated with research, development, and enhancement of proprietary computer software systems are expensed as incurred ($1.1 million in 1983).

5. ANACOMP, INC.
a. $109.6 million
b. $211.7 million
c. 6/30/82
d. Coopers & Lybrand

Software systems for commercial banks and thrift institutions.

Revenues are generally recognized as follows: (1) Data preparation, data processing, facility management, and computer output microfilm (COM) services and sales are recognized as the services are performed or products are shipped.
(2) Revenues from granting perpetual licenses of existing software systems which do not require substantial modification are recognized at the time the license agreement is executed; collectibility is reasonably assured, and the software system is delivered to the customer.
(3) Revenues from contracts for development and/or modifications to existing software systems are recognized under methods which approximate the percentage-of-completion method, except for revenues from development partnerships which are reported on the completed contract method, other than immaterial amounts reported for 1980. Losses on such contracts are recognized when identified.

Revenue recognized under items (2) and (3) may precede the date at which the customer may be billed pursuant to the contract terms. Substantially all unbilled revenue is collected in the year subsequent to the year revenue is recognized.

Purchased computer software systems held for licensing to others are carried at cost less accumulated depreciation. Depreciation is recorded over the estimated marketing lives of the software and is computed based on the greater of the amount calculated using either a percent-of-revenue or the straight-line method. The percent-of-revenue method is based on the total estimated future revenues expected to be derived from sales of the software, while straight-line depreciation is provided using estimated marketing lives of 5 to 10 years.

*(a) annual revenues, (b) total assets, (c) end of fiscal year, and (d) auditor.

Survey of Accounting Policies (continued)

Company*	Type of Product	Revenue Recognition Policy	Accounting Policy for Cost of Developed or Acquired Software
6. ANALYSTS INTER-NATIONAL CORPORATION *a.* $23.8 million *b.* $8.4 million *c.* 6/30/83 *d.* Touche Ross & Co.	Applications software; programming; systems analysis and design; consulting.	Not disclosed.	Not disclosed.
7. APOLLO COMPUTER, INC. *a.* $18 million *b.* $19.4 million *c.* 1/1/83 *d.* Arthur Andersen	Engineering, scientific and other technical applications systems.	Revenues from equipment and software sales are recognized upon shipment. Service revenues are recognized ratably over the contractual periods or as the services are provided.	All research and development costs, including costs for software development and enhancements to existing programs, are expensed as incurred.
8. APPLIED DATA RESEARCH, INC. *a.* $68.4 million *b.* $55.7 million *c.* 12/31/82 *d.* Peat, Marwick, Mitchell & Co.	Systems and applications software.	The company markets its products under lease agreements (generally 3 or 5 years) and permanent license agreements. Revenues are based on the present value of future payments and are recognized upon performance of the specific contract criteria (including product installation and customer acceptance) or upon execution of a noncancellable contract. Imputed finance charges are recognized as revenue over the terms of the respective contracts. All associated incremental costs are accrued in the period that such related revenue is recognized.	Purchased software costs are [capitalized and] amortized over a 10 year period. [The balance sheet discloses a net amount of $1.3 million at December 31, 1982.] All costs associated with development and enhancement of software products are charged to operations as incurred.

22

9. ASK COMPUTER SYSTEMS, INC.
  a. $39.4 million
  b. $38.9 million
  c. 6/30/83
  d. Arthur Young

Applications software; hardware.

Revenue from maintenance contracts, which cover periods of 1 to 3 years (1 to 4 years in 1981 and 1980), are based on the present value of future payments and are recognized upon execution of a noncancellable contract.

Maintenance services entitle a customer to receive future releases and enhancements of the related products. Such future releases and enhancements are a direct result of the company's ongoing research and development efforts and, accordingly, such costs are charged to earnings as accrued in the same period that related maintenance revenue is recognized.

Revenue is generally recognized upon product shipment, unless installation by the company is required prior to customer acceptance, in which case, revenue is recognized upon installation. Revenue from sublicense of the company's software by licensees is also required upon installation of the software.

Revenue from software subscription service, which includes updates to software products, is billed quarterly or annually, at which time revenue is recognized. Revenue from on-line remote processing service (ASKNET) and customer education is recognized as the services are provided. Net revenue includes $8,782,861, $5,301,522, and $1,996,504 in 1983, 1982, and 1981, respectively, from software subscription service, ASKNET, customer education, and

Software construction costs are expensed as incurred.

---

*(a) annual revenues, (b) total assets, (c) end of fiscal year, and (d) auditor.

23

Survey of Accounting Policies (continued)

Company*	Type of Product	Revenue Recognition Policy	Accounting Policy for Cost of Developed or Acquired Software
10. ASTRADYNE COMPUTER INDUSTRIES, INC. a. $8.6 million b. $4.1 million c. 12/31/82 d. Schwaeler Sloane Weitzman & Co.	Applications software systems and related services for banking and health care.	royalties, none of which accounted for more than 10 percent of net revenue in any year, except for ASKNET. ASKNET was 12 percent of net revenue in fiscal 1983, and the associated gross margin was 51 percent. Not disclosed.	Purchased program costs are included in property and equipment on the balance sheet and are disclosed by footnote. Amortization policy is not disclosed.
11. BPI SYSTEMS, INC. a. $6.1 million b. $7.1 million c. 3/31/83 d. Peat, Marwick, Mitchell & Co.	Application software for microcomputers.	Revenue from software development contracts is recognized under the terms of the agreements utilizing the percentage of completion method on an individual system basis. The percentage of completion is determined by the cost-to-cost method.	Research and development costs for new software applications are charged to operations when incurred.
12. BSL TECHNOLOGY a. $3.5 million b. $5 million	Medical clinical laboratory systems.	Revenues from contract sales are recognized on the percentage-of-completion method. Under percentage-of-completion accounting, contract revenue is accrued in the proportion that costs	Deferred software costs include production costs related to the enhancement or modification of an existing software product incurred

		incurred bear to the company's estimate of total contract costs. Losses are recorded in the period first identified and general and administrative expenses are charged to operations as incurred. Customers are billed according to the terms of the individual contracts. The finance method of accounting is used for lease receivables. Revenues are recognized over the term of the lease in decreasing amounts related to the declining balance of the receivable.	after the conceptualization and design of the product have been completed. These costs are deferred and amortized on a straight-line basis over the estimated period of benefit, but not to exceed three years. Such costs which are not reasonably assured of realization or which are deemed to have no future value are written off as software enhancement costs in excess of purchase commitments in the year this becomes apparent. Product development costs are charged to operations as incurred.
	c. 9/30/82 d. Touche Ross & Co.		
13. COMPUTER ASSOCIATES INTER-NATIONAL, INC. a. $58.1 million b. $50.7 million c. 3/31/83 d. Ernst & Whinney	Standardized systems software.	Product revenue is recognized upon installation and acceptance of the product by the customer. Installment accounts receivable resulting from product sales (perpetual and fixed-term licenses) with extended payment terms are discounted to present value using the rate estimated to be implicit in the contract. Maintenance fees (support fees) are recognized at the time the agreement becomes effective. Estimated future costs for software maintenance are provided based on agreements in force.	Cost of purchased software products are capitalized. Amortization is provided by the straight-line method over five years. [Net software is $5.4 million at 3/31/83.] Costs associated with development of and enhancements to software products are expensed as incurred.

*(a) annual revenues, (b) total assets, (c) end of fiscal year, and (d) auditor.

Survey of Accounting Policies (continued)

Company*	Type of Product	Revenue Recognition Policy	Accounting Policy for Cost of Developed or Acquired Software
14. COMPUTER DATA SYSTEMS. INC. *a.* $40.5 million *b.* $17.4 million *c.* 6/30/83 *d.* Deloitte Haskins & Sells	Processing services; applications software; consulting.	Revenues on time and material contracts are recorded at the contractual rates as the labor hours and out-of-pocket expenses are incurred. Revenues on cost-type contracts are recorded as reimbursable costs are incurred. Fixed fees are recorded on the percentage of completion basis, determined by the ratio of total incurred costs to anticipated total costs of the project. Revenues on unit-price contracts are recorded at contractual selling prices of work completed and accepted by the customer. Revenues on equipment and software sales are recorded when the units are delivered and installed. Immediate recognition is made of any anticipated losses.	Computer software programs which have been acquired and capitalized are amortized on the straight-line basis over their estimated useful lives of five years.
15. COMPUTER DESIGNED SYSTEMS. INC. *a.* $1.9 million *b.* $2.1 million *c.* 8/31/82 *d.* Coopers & Lybrand	Turnkey systems for medical clinical laboratories.	Revenues from sales of computer systems under noncancellable fixed price contracts are recognized under a percentage-of-completion method. Projected losses, if any, are recognized in their entirety in the current period without reference to percentage-of-completion. Revisions in costs and earnings during the course of the contract are reflected during the accounting period in which the facts become known. Revenue related to other services is recognized as the services are performed or products are delivered.	The company owns a library of proprietary software programs used in the design of customer systems. Costs related to the enhancement and improvement of existing programs or the purchase of new programs are capitalized and amortized over their estimated useful life of five to seven years. The costs of developing new proprietary software are expensed as incurred. Costs related to the

16. COMPUTER TASK GROUP, INC.
 a. $39.5 million
 b. $16.9 million
 c. 12/31/82
 d. Price Waterhouse

Software packages for the transportation industry and heavy equipment dealers; programming; systems engineering and analysis; services.

Revenue is recognized from services when the service has been provided. The company recognizes as revenue from software package license agreements 90 percent of the license fee upon execution of a noncancellable contract and the remaining 10 percent upon installation.

library of software deemed to have no future value are written off in the year this becomes apparent. Capitalized software costs include programmer salary costs of $173,007 in 1982, $162,079 in 1981, and $97,688 in 1980.

17. COMSERV CORPORATION
 a. $25 million
 b. $53.3 million
 c. 12/31/82
 d. Peat, Marwick, Mitchell & Co.

Applications software for manufacturing.

At the time of entering into licensing agreements for the use of proprietary software, the company recognizes the lesser of one half of the revenue or the nonrefundable portion of the agreement price paid by the customer at that time. The remainder of the agreement price is recognized as revenue upon effective delivery of the software. Revenue related to other services is recognized as the services are performed.

Not disclosed.

The company owns various proprietary computer software products that it licenses to customers and operates in its computer services facility. Certain costs related to the enhancement, improvement, and adaptation to particular requirements of the company's existing proprietary software are capitalized and are being amortized primarily on a straight-line basis over the estimated period of benefit, which is generally six years for software designed to operate on IBM-compatible mainframe computer

---

*(a) annual revenues. (b) total assets. (c) end of fiscal year, and (d) auditor.

Survey of Accounting Policies (continued)

Company*	Type of Product	Revenue Recognition Policy	Accounting Policy for Cost of Developed or Acquired Software
			equipment, and four years for all other software. The costs of purchased software are capitalized and amortized on the same basis. The costs incurred in the search for or evaluation of product or process alternatives or in the design of preproduction models or in conceptual formulation or translation of knowledge into designs for new or significantly improved software products are charged to research and development expense as incurred. Costs related to software deemed to have an impaired future value are written off immediately or amortized over the remaining estimated period of benefit once this becomes apparent. Net software construction costs amounted to $9,634,616 and $5,060,840 at December 31, 1982, and 1981, respectively. The company designs and constructs educational courseware that aids customers in effectively utilizing the company's software products.

18. COMSHARE, INCORPORATED a. $76.3 million b. $59.4 million c. 6/30/83 d. Arthur Andersen	Applications software.	Not disclosed.	These courseware construction costs are capitalized and are being amortized over the estimated period of benefit, which is four years. Net educational courseware construction costs amounted to $1,711,488 and $536,380 at December 31, 1982, and 1981, respectively. The cost of purchased software is capitalized and amortized on a straight-line basis over the lesser of 60 months or the expected life.... Research and development costs are charged to operations as incurred. [Net capitalized software is $1.5 million as of 6/30/83.]
19. CONSCO ENTERPRISES, INCORPORATED a. $1.6 million b. $1.5 million c. 12/31/82 d. Arthur Andersen	Financial applications software and support services.	Revenues are recognized over the life of the contract, normally a 12 month period. Sixty-five percent of software licensing revenues are recognized upon the signing of the contract, and the remaining 35 percent is recognized ratably over the life of the contract. Support agreement revenues are recognized at varying percentages upon contract signing and ratably over the remaining contract lives, depending on the level of support to be provided.	Costs to develop a software package are charged to expense currently. The company defers costs associated with the enhancement of existing software packages. Deferred costs include direct labor and computer costs. Amortization of deferred costs is charged to current operations on the straight-line method based on an estimated

*(a) annual revenues, (b) total assets, (c) end of fiscal year, and (d) auditor.

Survey of Accounting Policies (continued)

Company*	Type of Product	Revenue Recognition Policy	Accounting Policy for Cost of Developed or Acquired Software
20. THE CONTINUUM COMPANY, INC. *a.* $20.6 million *b.* $14.7 million *c.* 3/31/83 *d.* Ernst & Whinney	Applications software; service bureau.	Deferred Revenues represent the portion of contract revenues not yet recognized. The revenue recognition policy is designed to match the recording of income to the incurrence of the expenses associated with servicing the contract.	useful life of five years. For tax purposes, software development and enhancement costs have been expensed as incurred. Purchased computer programs are carried at cost less accumulated amortization. Amortization is provided evenly over the estimated useful lives of the programs, generally five years. [Net amount of $175,000 appears in the 3/31/83 balance sheet.] The costs of developing and improving computer programs are charged to expense as incurred. Some of these costs are funded by revenue received from customers.
21. COOK DATA SERVICES, INC. *a.* $6.1 million *b.* $2.8 million *c.* 12/31/82 *d.* Kenneth Leventhal & Company	Applications software for oil and gas.	Revenue from a license sale is recorded when the software product licensed is deliverable. Revenue from systems installation charges, computer processing fees, education, and consulting are recognized as services are performed and are billed at contractual rates. Deferred revenue consists primarily of advances on certain software and on installation contracts. The advances are recognized as revenue upon the completion of specific contractual events. Customers are billed at the end of each month for actual usage of the various programs and the company recognizes such revenues when billed. Certain customers license one or more of the programs for use on their own computer equipment. These customers pay a one-time fee for use of the program, and this fee is recognized as revenue upon delivery. The company has no obligation to provide programming changes made subsequent to the licensing, unless the	The costs associated with developing new program applications and enhancements to existing applications are treated as research and development costs and expensed as incurred. Costs incurred to develop computer programs, which include wages and computer usage and supplies, without any contractual

22. CULLINET SOFTWARE
    a. $78.6 million
    b. $107.1 million
    c. 4/30/83
    d. Tonneson, Mela, Curtin & Company [Wakefield, Mass.]

Database management systems; applications software.

customer enters an agreement whereby it pays a monthly fee to the company for the right to receive such program enhancements. These fees are reported as revenue monthly as billed. The company also normally agrees to provide support services for a period of time to purchasers of its programs. Those services are billed to the customers and revenues recognized as the services are rendered.

The company recognizes revenue from the initial "license to use" computer software upon the delivery and acceptance of the programs by the customer. A license to use is issued for a period of one year. After the initial term of the license, an annual renewal fee is charged. Certain contracts allow the customer to pay the initial license fee in monthly installments over a period of from one to five years with interest and administrative fees, at varying rates, charged on the unpaid balance.

Discounts to foreign representatives. The company utilizes foreign representatives to market and provide technical support for its products in various parts of the world. As part of the agreements with the foreign representatives, the company gives discounts that are typically 55 percent of the list price of the products licensed through the foreign representatives. The company classifies the discounts as a reduction of revenue.

arrangements with customers, are charged to expense as research and development costs. Such costs approximated $70,000 in 1980, $190,000 in 1981, and $360,000 in 1982.

Purchased computer software licenses. The costs to acquire licenses of certain computer software products and product lines are being amortized on the straight-line method over the estimated economic lives of the assets, which currently range from 5 to 10 years. Certain provisions of the license agreements require royalty payments when the company recognizes revenue from licensing the products to its customers.

Purchased computer software licenses are shown net of accumulated amortization of $1,273,000 and $312,000 at April 30, 1983 and 1982, respectively. Research, development, and installation costs are charged to expense as incurred.

---

*(a) annual revenues, (b) total assets, (c) end of fiscal year, and (d) auditor.

Survey of Accounting Policies (continued)

Company*	Type of Product	Revenue Recognition Policy	Accounting Policy for Cost of Developed or Acquired Software
23. CYCARE SYSTEMS, INC. a. $23.5 million b. $15.3 million c. 12/31/82 d. Price Waterhouse	Applications software for the medical profession.	The company is in one line of business which consists of providing information processing services, including the incidental sale of equipment and the licensing of related software for such information processing, primarily to physicians and medical group practices throughout the United States and Canada. Revenues are recognized for financial statement purposes when the related service is provided and upon shipment of equipment and software.	Research and development costs, principally the design and development of proprietary systems and programming, are expensed as incurred. Routine maintenance of proprietary software is also expensed as incurred. The company purchased the exclusive rights to a software license in 1981 for licensing to physicians and medical group practices. The cost of the software license will be amortized over a seven-year period. [Balance of $791,000 at 12/31/82.]
24. DST SYSTEMS, INC. a. $37.5 million b. $42.1 million c. 12/31/82 d. Price Waterhouse	Software systems for the mutual fund industry.	Revenue is recognized upon completion of services performed.	Software research, development, and maintenance costs are expensed as incurred. Research and development costs were $16,000, $1,097,000, and $1,566,000 for the years ended December 31, 1980, 1981, and 1982, respectively.
25. DATA ARCHITECTS, INC.	Custom software; applications software for banking industry.	The company recognizes revenue from consulting services as they are rendered. Revenues from software product license agreements are	Licensed software (acquired) is amortized over five years using the straight-line method beginning in

a. $12.6 million
b. $8.6 million
c. 11/30/82
d. Deloitte Haskins and Sells

recognized in accordance with the payment terms of agreement: 30 percent of the fee upon execution of a contract and the remaining 70 percent upon installation and customer acceptance.

the year in which product sales are first made.

26. DYATRON CORPORATION

Service bureau; applications software.

a. $33 million
b. $30 million
c. 12/31/82
d. Coopers & Lybrand

Data processing revenues are recognized in the period for which the service is provided. Rental revenue from the leasing of terminals is recognized using the operating method. Software license revenues are recognized when the contract is signed, a deposit has been received, and delivery of the tapes and manuals is scheduled within 90 days from the contract date. Fees related to support agreements for software packages are recognized at the time of receipt of the fee in cash or if earlier upon receipt of executed agreements; estimated incremental expenses directly related to the contracts are accrued on a current basis. Receipts of license fees for software packages under development are recorded as deferred revenue and are recognized when the packages become deliverable. General and administrative expense includes $318,000, $380,000, and $922,000 as a provision for doubtful accounts in 1982, 1981, and 1980, respectively.

Research and development (R&D) costs are expensed as incurred. (R&D activities include the search for new knowledge, the translation of new or other knowledge into a plan or design for a new or significantly improved product, and the conceptual formulation, design, and testing of product alternatives. Most of the company's R&D activities relate to development of new computer software which is used in producing new services.) Also expensed as incurred are computer software maintenance and enhancement costs and the costs of developing special software under cost reimbursement contracts.

Other costs applicable in the development of software obtained for the purpose of producing a new product or service for sale to customers are capitalized and

*(a) annual revenues, (b) total assets, (c) end of fiscal year, and (d) auditor.

Survey of Accounting Policies (continued)

Company*	Type of Product	Revenue Recognition Policy	Accounting Policy for Cost of Developed or Acquired Software
			amortized over the estimated useful life of the software, generally five to seven years, using the straight-line method. These costs consist primarily of the purchase price of externally purchased programs, the programming, debugging, and documentation costs for internally developed programs and the costs of developing the related operating procedures. [Balance sheet indicates $2.2 million (net) at 12/31/83.]
27. HARRIS & PAULSON, INC. *a.* $1.2 million *b.* $1.8 million *c.* 9/30/82 *d.* Fleming, Tempas & Company [Englewood, Colorado]	Applications software for the legal profession.	Revenue is derived from licensing the use of a software system and the sale of related hardware (system sales) and providing an in-house time sharing service bureau (data processing services). System sales revenue is generally recognized when a sales contract is executed with the customer; installation of the related hardware and software is accomplished in a reasonable time; and, substantially all costs to complete the sale and installation have been incurred or accrued. Data processing services revenue is recognized when the related services are provided.	Costs relating to the enhancement, which result in the betterment of existing software, are capitalized. Research and development cost are charged to expense as incurred. [Software is $285,000 at 9/30/82.]

28. HOGAN SYSTEMS, INC.
a. $17 million
b. $28.2 million
c. 3/31/83
d. Price Waterhouse

Applications software for the banking industry.

Under current contracts the company recognizes revenue from the licensing of previously marketed software programs upon delivery of documentation and recognizes revenue from contracts for the licensing of programs under development when the programs are delivered. Previously, some of the company's contracts required the customer to make one or more nonrefundable progress payments but gave the customer the right to cancel the purchase and discontinue further payments at any time. Revenue from these contracts is recognized as payments are received. Also, some contracts required the customer to make one or more nonrefundable progress payments with final payment upon acceptance. For these contracts, the progress payments are recognized as revenue after delivery of the software, and the final payment is recognized upon acceptance. Both initial and renewal maintenance contracts are of one-year duration and revenue is recognized ratably over the maintenance contract term. Revenue from customer training and installation support is recognized upon completion of the service provided. Reimbursement by customers under participation agreements are included in revenues in the period in which the related costs are incurred. These participation agreements represent contributions by customers to the

The cost of purchased software is capitalized and depreciated on the straight-line basis over five-year periods. Development costs incurred by the company are expensed as incurred.

---

*(a) annual revenues, (b) total assets, (c) end of fiscal year, and (d) auditor.

Survey of Accounting Policies (continued)

Company*	Type of Product	Revenue Recognition Policy	Accounting Policy for Cost of Developed or Acquired Software
29. INFODATA SYSTEMS, INC. a. $6.5 million b. $4.2 million c. 12/31/82 d. Ernst & Whinney	Off-the-shelf computer programs.	development of specific software systems. The agreements include a provision for the customers to recover, solely from a royalty on the licensing of the developed software to unrelated parties, all or a portion of amounts contributed. Revenues relating to licensing of the company's established software products are generally recognized at the time of entering into licensing agreements or upon receipt of other appropriate documentation supporting a binding agreement to purchase. Revenue from consulting services is recognized on the percentage-of-completion method for fixed-price agreements and on the basis of hours incurred at contract rates for time and material agreements. Revenues associated with license agreements with payment terms which extend beyond one year are discounted to their present value. Revenues associated with customer maintenance agreements are recognized on a monthly basis. The cost of such maintenance support is recorded as incurred.	Costs associated with the enhancement or modification of existing software products for the purpose of creating new features are capitalized. Through 1981, such costs were amortized over the anticipated period of future benefit, but not in excess of seven years. During 1982, management determined that amortization of these costs over a five year period from the date the software is placed in service would provide a better matching of revenues and related expenses. The effect of this change in estimate is not material to 1982 income or earnings per share. The effect of this change on future years' operations is not determinable, because it will be dependent upon the amount of future expenditures.

30. INFORMATICS GENERAL CORPORATION

a. $170.2 million
b. $92.7 million
c. 12/31/82
d. Deloitte Haskins & Sells

Systems and applications software; consulting; processing services.

Revenue from sales of software products results from agreements which provide customers the right to use these products on a perpetual or fixed term basis. Such revenues are generally recognized based upon the execution of the agreement and delivery of the product to the customer which, in certain cases, involves the use of the percentage-of-completion method of accounting based on progress toward installation.

Revenue from "Professional Services" is recognized as earned, which in the case of certain contracts involves the use of the percentage-of-completion method of accounting.

Revenue from "Information Processing Services" is recognized in the period in which such services are rendered. When products and services are billed prior to the time the related revenue is earned, deferred revenues are recorded.

Research and product development expenses represent the costs of designing, developing, and testing new software and other computer-related products. These costs include amounts expended to develop products for which the company has issued advance license agreements to customers. Revenue related to these license agreements is recognized on the percentage-of-completion method of accounting.

Costs of software products purchased from outsiders or acquired through business combinations are deferred and amortized over the lesser of the projected term of the related revenue or five years, using the straight-line method.

All software development costs are expensed as incurred.

31. INTEGRATED SOFTWARE SYSTEMS CORPORATION

a. $16.6 million
b. $11.6 million
c. 12/31/82
d. Deloitte Haskins & Sells

Software for graphic applications.

The company recognizes 60 percent of the revenue from issuance of a perpetual license to use its software upon signing of an agreement and shipment of the related software; 40 percent is recognized upon completion of installation.

Revenue from the rental of computer software programs is recognized ratably over the period of the lease agreements.

Income from annual maintenance and enhancement fees is recognized ratably over the periods covered by such agreements.

---

*(a) annual revenues, (b) total assets, (c) end of fiscal year, and (d) auditor.

Survey of Accounting Policies (continued)

Company*	Type of Product	Revenue Recognition Policy	Accounting Policy for Cost of Developed or Acquired Software
32. INTERMETRICS, INC. a. $24.3 million b. $10.3 million c. 2/28/82 d. Arthur Andersen	Software production tools; applications and systems engineering software for the space, defense, and aviation industries; industrial productivity monitoring and control systems.	The company recognizes revenue on government and commercial contracts under the percentage-of-completion method. The percentage-of-completion is determined by relating the cost incurred to date to the estimated total cost in order to measure the stage of completion. The cumulative effects resulting from revisions of estimated total contract costs and revenues are recorded in the period in which the facts requiring revision become known. When a loss is anticipated on a contract, the full amount thereof is provided currently. The amounts shown as unbilled costs and fees on contracts in process represent the excess of expenditures on contracts, plus profits or less losses recorded thereon, over billings to date. Billings made on contracts are recorded as a reduction of unbilled costs and fees, and to the extent that such billings exceed costs incurred, they are recorded as unearned revenue.	Not disclosed.
33. LODGISTIX, INC. a. $5.5 million b. $5.4 million c. 6/30/83 d. Arthur Young	Applications software for hotel industry (reservations).	Not disclosed.	Costs applicable to the development of software obtained for the purpose of producing a new product or service for sale to customers are capitalized and amortized over the estimated useful life of the software—generally, three to five years using

38

the straight-line method. These costs consist primarily of the purchase price of externally purchased programs, the programming, debugging, and documentation costs for internally developed programs and the costs of developing the related operating procedures. Computer software maintenance and minor enhancement costs are expensed as incurred. [Net software is $643,807 at 6/30/83.]

At June 30, 1983, the company's unamortized costs for internally developed computer software costs was $588,165. The company has capitalized internal software development costs during the past three years as follows:

	1983	1982	1981
Capitalized costs	$300,176	$149,940	$127,072
Amortization	222,196	156,000	145,484
Net capitalized costs	$ 77,980	$ (6,060)	$(18,412)

---

*(a) annual revenues, (b) total assets, (c) end of fiscal year, and (d) auditor.

Survey of Accounting Policies (continued)

Company*	Type of Product	Revenue Recognition Policy	Accounting Policy for Cost of Developed or Acquired Software
34. MACNEAL-SCHWENDLER CORPORATION a. $9.2 million b. $5.2 million c. 1/31/83 d. Arthur Young	Software for computer-aided engineering.	Revenues from leasing computer-software products are recognized monthly as earned. The software leases generally provide for a monthly minimum rental with additional amounts due based on usage.	Research and development costs relate to designing, developing, and testing new or significantly improved software products and include an allocation of general and administrative expenses.
35. MANAGEMENT SCIENCE AMERICA, INC. a. $101.2 million b. $76.3 million c. 12/31/82 d. Price Waterhouse	Applications software.	The company recognizes 90 percent of the license fees from mainframe software package agreements upon execution of the contract and the remaining 10 percent upon installation of the software package. Microcomputer-software license fees are recognized upon shipment of the product or upon execution of an agreement. Revenues related to long-term contracts to develop microcomputer software for hardware manufacturers are recognized on the percentage-of-completion method of accounting. Fees related to support agreements for software packages are recognized at the time of receipt of the fee in cash or, if earlier, upon receipt of an executed agreement; estimated incremental expenses directly related to the support of customers under such agreements are accrued on a current basis. The company has established an allowance for returns and doubtful accounts of $4,295,000, $2,295,000, and $1,527,000 at December 31, 1982, 1981, and 1980, respectively.	The cost of software packages purchased from outsiders or acquired through business combinations is amortized using the straight-line method over periods not exceeding seven years for financial reporting purposes and five years for income tax purposes. All costs associated with development and enhancement of software products are expensed as incurred.

36. MATHEMATICA, INC.
a. $36 million
b. $21 million
c. 6/30/82
d. Arthur Andersen

Contracted services; systems software. (Subsequently acquired by Martin Marietta Corporation.)

Revenue from professional service activities is primarily derived from projects, and is recognized on a percentage-of-completion basis by relating the actual cost of work performed to date to the current estimated total cost of the respective projects. When estimates indicate a probable ultimate loss on a project, the full amount thereof is recognized.

Proprietary database management systems are generally marketed under long-term, noncancellable license arrangements. The present value of license payments are recognized as revenue upon commencement of the licensing agreements, and the imputed finance charges are recorded as earned revenues over the term of the contracts. Annual maintenance support fees, which are not refundable, are recognized as revenue on the anniversary date of the licensing agreement.

All costs associated with research, design, development, and documentation of new products, as well as the enhancement of existing products—including allocable indirect costs—are expensed as incurred.

37. McCORMACK & DODGE CORP.
a. $26.2 million
b. $15.8 million
c. 12/31/81
d. Main Hurdman

Applications software for the finance industry. (Subsequently acquired by Dun & Bradstreet.)

Revenue from the licensing of previously marketed software programs is recognized upon execution of a contract. Revenues from contracts for the licensing of programs under development are recognized when the program has become deliverable. At the time income is recorded, future costs associated with the sale are fully provided. Enhancement revenue is recorded ratably over the life of the contract.

All costs associated with program development, continuing maintenance, and support of existing software packages are expensed as incurred.

---

*(a) annual revenues, (b) total assets, (c) end of fiscal year, and (d) auditor.

Survey of Accounting Policies (continued)

Company*	Type of Product	Revenue Recognition Policy	Accounting Policy for Cost of Developed or Acquired Software
38. MICRO-SOFTWARE INTER-NATIONAL, INC. a. $508,000 b. $676,000 c. 9/30/82 d. McGladrey Hendrickson & Co.	Applications software for microcomputers.	Revenue is recognized upon installation of the respective computerized hardware system or software package.	Research and development costs, consisting primarily of salaries paid to programmers who develop the company's software package, are expensed as incurred.
39. MILLER TECHNOLOGY & COMMUNI-CATIONS CORP. a. $7.7 million b. $10.8 million c. 9/30/82 d. Pannell, Kerr, Foster	Systems hardware and software for educational institutions.	Revenue from the sale of hardware is recognized when shipped. Revenue from the licensing of proprietary software is recognized based upon delivery of the product to the customer, which in certain cases, may involve use of the percentage-of-completion method of accounting.	Computer software costs are included in "other assets." Enhancement and improvement costs are deferred and amortized over five years.
40. THE MPSI GROUP, INC. a. $14.3 million b. $15.6 million c. 9/30/83 d. Peat, Marwick, Mitchell & Co.	Applications software and related data bases for petroleum companies and other multi-outlet retailers.	The company allows certain customers to utilize its computer software under multi-year license contracts. Revenue on these long-term software user agreements is recognized at the time the contract becomes effective. There are no future direct costs associated with these agreements, since monthly computer usage charges and	Developed computer software costs are reflected at a nominal value in the financial statements in order to give recognition to a significant earning asset. The reported value is not intended to reflect actual costs which are expensed annually

| 41. MTX INTER-NATIONAL, INC.
a. $525 thousand
b. $1 million
c. 9/30/83
d. Arthur Young | Software and hardware microcomputer products to construction contractors; management and technical consulting services. | training fees (if any) are passed on to the customer. The revenue and corresponding long-term receivables related to these contracts are stated at the present value of the payments to be received over the contract term (normally five years). The present value is determined using the prime rate applicable to the company on the effective date of the contract. The discount related to the amounts maturing in excess of one year is amortized to income on an accelerated method that produces level interest earnings based on the outstanding balance. Revenue is recognized on software/hardware products upon shipment to the customer. Revenue from consulting and other services is recognized at the time the services are performed or ratably over the term of maintenance contracts. Revenue from the granting of exclusive dealerships is recognized when the fees are due. | as the software is developed and are significantly greater than the recorded amount. Research and development costs relating to developing new proprietary software are expensed as incurred. Costs associated with the purchase of marketable software and the addition of features or capabilities which enhance the product are deferred and are being amortized on a straight-line basis over the estimated period of benefit, which is five years. |
| 42. NCA CORPORATION
a. $12.8 million
b. $14 million | Applications software. | The company uses the percentage-of-completion method for recognizing revenue of Computer Aided Design (CAD) software packages in progress, which in some cases can require up to | Not disclosed. [No capitalized software is apparent in the balance sheet; appears to be expensed as incurred.] |

*(a) annual revenues, (b) total assets, (c) end of fiscal year, and (d) auditor.

Survey of Accounting Policies (continued)

Company*	Type of Product	Revenue Recognition Policy	Accounting Policy for Cost of Developed or Acquired Software
c. 12/31/82 d. Price Waterhouse		four months to convert and install. The company recognizes revenue for its manufacturing and financial computer software packages at the time of installation; such packages generally require less than one month to install. In addition, the company enters into one year software maintenance contracts, which include software enhancements, at the time of software installation. Revenue from these contracts, which are renewable on an annual basis, is recognized on a straight-line basis over the term of the contract.	
43. ON-LINE SOFTWARE INTERNATIONAL, INC. a. $20.2 million b. $16.3 million c. 5/31/83 d. Ernst & Whinney	IBM systems software.	Revenue is derived from licensing the use of software products, providing ongoing maintenance with regard to software product licenses, and providing consulting and education services. Revenue is recognized from consulting and education when the related service is provided. Revenue related to software products is generally recognized after a licensee has agreed to accept the product; licensee acceptance usually follows a 30 day trial period. Maintenance agreements are sold for one-year periods beginning on the first anniversary of the license agreement, and revenue is recognized upon sale. Education services are billed to customers in advance of the date of the course of instruction.	All costs related to the development of software products are charged to expense as incurred. The cost of proprietary software purchased from outsiders is amortized over its useful life or five years, whichever is shorter. [The balance sheet indicates $1,681,000 in purchased software at 5/31/83.] Purchased proprietary software has been recorded at cost based upon purchase agreements for the proprietary products. The agreements provide for the company to pay commissions averaging approximately 15 to 20

44

percent of revenue derived from the sale of these products. The cost of purchased proprietary software has been reduced by $44,000 of accumulated amortization.

Costs of product development are charged to income as incurred. [Purchased software is recorded at cost and is being amortized] on a basis related to estimated revenues for the seven years following the purchase. [Net purchased software is $8.1 million at 4/30/83.]

The cost of software research and development by the company is charged to expense as incurred. The amounts charged were $11,875,000, $6,763,000, and $4,441,000 in 1982, 1981, and 1980, respectively.

Accordingly, such advance billings are recorded as deferred revenue.

Revenue from perpetual license agreements, leases, rentals, and installment sales are recognized upon shipment of the product, receipt of a signed contract, and acceptance by the customer. Revenues from customer-support agreements are recognized when billed. Lease revenues are recorded at the fair value of an equivalent perpetual license at the date of the contract; additional amounts due under lease agreements—principally finance charges—are recorded as earned revenues over the term of the contract.

Systems licensing agreements generally have an initial fee (presently called an Initial License Charge) and a monthly fee (presently called a Monthly License Charge). The monthly charge is adequate to cover, among other things, all continuing costs to be incurred by the company as a result of the license agreement and provide a normal profit. The monthly charge is recorded and recognized as revenue on a monthly basis throughout the term of the license agreements. The initial charge is recognized as revenue at the time the license agreement is executed. Earlier agreements provided for installment payments of

44. PANSOPHIC SYSTEMS, INC.
a. $43.1 million
b. $33.1 million
c. 4/30/83
d. Price Waterhouse

Systems and applications software.

45. POLICY MANAGEMENT SYSTEMS CORPORATION
a. $44.5 million
b. $43.3 million
c. 9/30/82
d. Clarkson, Harden and Gantt [Columbia, South Carolina]

Applications software for the insurance industry.

---

*(a) annual revenues, (b) total assets, (c) end of fiscal year, and (d) auditor.

45

Survey of Accounting Policies (continued)

Company*	Type of Product	Revenue Recognition Policy	Accounting Policy for Cost of Developed or Acquired Software
		the initial charge, and the revenue amounts were discounted at then current interest rates, and, in some instances, a deferment of the initial charge, with monthly charges for such deferment. Services revenues are recognized monthly as the services are performed. Advance payments for services are recorded as unearned revenue and not recognized as revenue until the performance of such services.	
46. SCIENCE MANAGEMENT CORPORATION a. $46.5 million b. $23.7 million c. 12/31/82 d. Price Waterhouse	Management services; consulting; systems design.	The company generally recognizes income from professional service and construction contracts on the percentage-of-completion method. The percentage-of-completion is determined at the end of an accounting period by the ratio of time expended to management's estimate of total time required for each project. The percentage, so determined, is applied to the total contract fee, and the resultant amount is compared with the amount billed. The excess of fees earned over amounts billed is reported as unbilled receivables. The excess of billings over fees earned is included in accounts payable and accrued expenses.	Costs of developing new proprietary computer software products are expensed as incurred. Costs related to the improvement and enhancement of existing computer software and the adaptation of such software for use on other computer equipment are deferred. Deferred costs are amortized on a straight-line basis over the estimated period of benefit (not to exceed three years) or are written-off in the year a particular software system is deemed to have no future value. Unamortized software construction costs of $969,000 and $550,000 are included in other assets at December 31, 1982, and 1981, respectively.

47. SCIENTIFIC SOFTWARE CORP.
a. $17.5 million
b. $18.1 million
c. 12/31/82
d. Price Waterhouse

Applications software for the petroleum industry; processing; consulting.

Proprietary software programs are licensed to customers for either a 99-year term or on a short-term basis (for periods of 1 to 5 years). Revenues from 99-year licenses are generally recorded in accordance with the timing of the obligations set forth in the executed license agreement. Revenues from the first year of a short-term license are recorded in full when the license is executed. Revenues subsequent to the first year of a short-term license are recorded annually on the renewal dates.

Revenues on time and material contracts are recorded at the contractual rates as the labor hours and associated costs and expenses are incurred. Fixed-price contract revenues are recorded over the term of the project based on the percentage-of-completion method of accounting.

The company expenses, as incurred, the costs of developing proprietary computer programs. [The company is also developing software as a general partner in a research and development partnership arrangement.]

48. SCIENTIFIC SYSTEMS SERVICES, INC.
a. $15.5 million
b. $9.6 million
c. 12/31/82
d. Deloitte Haskins & Sells

Software and systems for electric utilities and industry.

Revenue on time and material contracts is recognized as time is expended and costs are incurred. Revenues from fixed-price contracts are recognized on the percentage-of-completion method, measured by the percentage of labor and overhead costs incurred to date to total estimated labor and overhead costs for each contract.

Research and development costs are expensed as incurred. Costs from fixed-price contracts are recognized on the percentage-of-completion basis, measured by the percentage of labor and overhead costs incurred to date to total estimated labor and overhead costs for each contract. Costs incurred, but not recognized, are deferred and recognized under the

---

*(a) annual revenues, (b) total assets, (c) end of fiscal year, and (d) auditor.

Survey of Accounting Policies (continued)

Company*	Type of Product	Revenue Recognition Policy	Accounting Policy for Cost of Developed or Acquired Software
49. SENTRY DATA, INC. a. $876,000 b. $853,000 c. 12/31/82 d. Peat, Marwick, Mitchell & Co.	Hospital information systems and software.	Hospital systems revenue is recognized on a completed-contract-segment basis as installation of each respective systems segment is completed. Respective services revenue is derived from services rendered on an hourly basis and is recognized as services are rendered. Such revenue includes systems installation, when contracted for on an hourly basis, as well as ongoing systems maintenance.	Expensed as incurred. percentage-of-completion method over the remaining contract period.
50. SOFTECH, INC. a. $35.5 million b. $23.9 million c. 5/31/83 d. Coopers & Lybrand	Custom applications software; standard software packages.	Income from contracts is recognized on the percentage-of-completion basis. Percentage of completion is determined by relating the actual cost of work performed to date for each contract to its current estimated final cost. If a loss is indicated by the estimate to complete a contract, a provision is made for the entire loss in the current period. The amounts shown as unbilled costs and fees on contracts in progress represent the excess expenditures (including overhead and general and administrative costs) on contracts, plus profits or less losses recorded thereon, over billings to date. Nonrefundable license fees are recorded as revenue upon execution of the license	Software development costs are charged to expense as incurred.

51. SOFTWARE AG SYSTEMS GROUP, INC.

a. $30 million
b. $36 million
c. 5/31/83
d. Peat, Marwick, Mitchell & Co.

Systems software.

The company sells, or leases under arrangements equivalent to a sale, a license to use its systems software products. Revenue is recognized when the contract is executed. Ten percent of the price is deferred and reflected in revenues when the product is installed. In contracts where the terms indicate a sale upon the satisfaction of other criteria, such as acceptance upon approval, revenue recognition is delayed until those specific terms are met. Maintenance fees received from customers are recorded as revenue when billed.

Royalty fees are recorded as revenue based upon sales by the licensee. The company defers a portion of the revenue received under certain license agreements. The portion deferred represents the company's estimate of the cost of maintenance support and is amortized into income over the maintenance support period.

All costs associated with development and improvement of software products are charged to operations as incurred. [The company has capitalized license rights to certain software which is being amortized over approximately seven years. The net license is $5.5 million at May 31, 1983.]

52. STERLING SOFTWARE, INC.

a. $3.1 million
b. $3.5 million
c. 9/30/82
d. Arthur Young

Systems software; banking applications software.

Revenue and royalties from software system sales are recognized upon delivery of the system and/or acceptance of the product by the customer. Revenues from maintenance and enhancement fees are recognized at the inception of the maintenance period. Related costs of maintenance and enhancement contracts are estimated based upon the length of the contract and accrued in total when the related revenues are recognized.

Purchased software is depreciated on a straight-line basis over five years. Research and development costs relating to designing, developing, and testing new or significantly improved software products are expensed as incurred.

---

*(a) annual revenues, (b) total assets, (c) end of fiscal year, and (d) auditor.

Survey of Accounting Policies (continued)

Company*	Type of Product	Revenue Recognition Policy	Accounting Policy for Cost of Developed or Acquired Software
53. SYSTEMATICS. INC. *a.* $64.4 million *b.* $52.8 million *c.* 5/31/83 *d.* Price Waterhouse	Data processing centers for banks; applications software packages for the banking industry.	Data processing revenue is recognized as services are performed. A portion of the revenue from the company's software license agreements is deferred to provide for costs to be incurred subsequent to the execution of the contract, such as documentation and installation costs and an appropriate profit thereon. Annual maintenance fee revenue associated with software license agreements is recognized on a monthly basis.	Software purchased by the company and utilized in providing electronic data processing services is capitalized and amortized on a straight-line basis over five years. Costs related to the development and maintenance of the company's software systems are charged to operations as incurred. [Net amount of $232,900 is indicated in 5/31/83 balance sheet.]
54. SYSTEMS & COMPUTER TECHNOLOGY CORPORATION *a.* $43.8 million *b.* $14.2 million *c.* 9/30/83 *d.* Ernst & Whinney	Applications software for higher education and local government markets.	The company provides computer-related services under computing sources management contracts, including provision of company developed applications software, and in connection with software licensing agreements, for institutions of higher education and local governments and agencies. Work is performed in general under contracts which provide for fees based on a multiple applied to employees' compensation and reimbursements of certain expenses. Such reimbursements are classified as reduction of other operating expenses in the accompanying statements of income. Revenue is accrued as work is performed in accordance	Not disclosed. [No capitalized software costs are apparent in the balance sheet.]

with the term of the related contracts. Contracts generally provide for service to be performed by the company over a period of years. Certain contracts include a billing schedule which provides for billings in the year subsequent to the year in which services are performed. Such contracts provide for interest on the excess of accrued revenues over billings. Other revenues accrued in excess of billings represent amounts attributable to normal large lags between the performance of work and the related subsequent billing.

The company also licenses its applications software under agreements which provide for a one-time license fee for which the client receives a perpetual nontransferable, nonexclusive right to use the software. Revenue from one-time license fees is generally recorded upon execution of the licensing agreement

Research and development costs primarily for the development of software products are charged to operations as incurred. The costs approximated $877,000, $795,000, and $700,000 for the years ended May 31, 1983, 1982, and 1981, respectively.

55. **TIME SHARING RESOURCES, INC.**
   a. $13.4 million
   b. $7.7 million
   c. 5/31/83
   d. Peat, Marwick, Mitchell & Co.

Systems and applications software.

Not disclosed.

---

*(a) annual revenues, (b) total assets, (c) end of fiscal year, and (d) auditor.

Survey of Accounting Policies (concluded)

Company*	Type of Product	Revenue Recognition Policy	Accounting Policy for Cost of Developed or Acquired Software
56. WYLY CORPORATION (University Computing) a. $165.8 million b. $114.4 million c. 12/31/82 d. Arthur Young	Computing services; systems and applications software; "turnkey" minicomputer systems.	[Deferred income.] Deferred income consists primarily of software maintenance and billed software contracts which have not been recognized in revenue. Maintenance revenue is recognized ratably over the maintenance period. Revenue from billed software is recognized when the software is delivered.	Purchased software is amortized by the straight-line method over the period expected to be benefited, which is generally five years. [Balance sheet at 12/31/82 indicates $7.8 million (net) in purchased software.]

*(a) annual revenues, (b) total assets, (c) end of fiscal year, and (d) auditor.

CHAPTER 3

Survey of Software Vendors

Introduction

This chapter summarizes the mail questionnaire responses that were received from 88 private and public software vending companies.[1]

QUESTION 1

What amortization method and time period range are used for *financial statement purposes* to amortize: (1) purchased software intended for: (*a*) internal use or (*b*) resale: (2) internally developed software intended for: (*a*) internal use or (*b*) sale?

This question attempted to determine the percentage of software-vendor companies that capitalize certain categories of software expenditure. The responses to this question also revealed the amortization methods used and the estimated asset life, by catagory.

Based on the responses, it can tentatively be concluded that:

1. For software purchased for internal use:
   a. A majority of both private (57 percent) and public (73 percent) companies capitalize these software costs.
   b. Public companies are more likely to capitalize these costs than are privately held companies.
   c. The vast majority of the capitalized software (75.9 percent or more) is amortized over five years or less.
   d. The straight-line method is by far the most frequently used method (96.6 percent).

2. For software purchased for resale:
   a. Slightly over half (55 percent) of publicly held companies capitalize this type of software, but less than one in three (32 percent) privately held companies do so.
   b. Public companies are more likely to capitalize these costs than are privately held companies.
   c. The vast majority of the capitalized software (85.0 percent or more) in this category is amortized over five years or less.
   d. The straight-line method is by far the most frequently used method (82.5 percent).
3. For software constructed for internal use:
   a. The vast majority of both private (97 percent) and public (92 percent) companies expense such software.
   b. Public companies appear to be slightly more likely to capitalize (8 percent) than private companies (3 percent).
   c. The majority of capitalized software (60 percent) is amortized over eight years or less.
   d. The straight-line method is by far (100 percent) the most frequently used method.
4. For software constructed for sale:
   a. The vast majority of both private (78 percent) and public (90 percent) companies expense such software.
   b. Private companies appear to be slightly more likely to capitalize (22 percent) than public companies (10 percent).
   c. The vast majority of the capitalized software (at least 69.2 percent) in this category is amortized over five years or less.
   d. The straight-line method is by far the most frequently used method (61.5 percent).
5. Purchased software is capitalized more frequently than is internally constructed software.
6. Public companies are more likely to capitalize software costs than private companies.
7. Most software is amortized over five years or less.
8. The straight-line method is by far the most frequently used method.

QUESTION 2

How are software costs classified on the balance sheet?
   The responses to this question revealed that:

1. Software assets used internally, whether purchased or constructed internally, are most likely to appear on the balance sheet as:
   a. A fixed asset without separate disclosure.
   b. A specific noncurrent asset line item.
2. Software assets intended for sale, whether purchased or internally constructed, are likely to be listed as a specific noncurrent asset line item.

QUESTION 3

Software costs appearing on the balance sheet represent what percent of total assets?

Software costs appearing on the balance sheet represented less than 5 percent of total assets for about 70 percent of the companies responding to this question. If materiality is defined as 5 percent of total assets, then software assets are a material item for 31 percent of the companies in this survey. If materiality is defined as 10 percent, then the item is material for 15 percent of the companies. For one private and public company, the percentages were 76.8 and 68.0, respectively.

QUESTION 4

What costs are capitalized for internally developed software that is intended for: (1) internal use; (2) sale.

Responses to this question reveal that the categories of costs most frequently capitalized are design, coding, and testing costs. Software construction costs were more likely to be capitalized if the software was intended for sale than if it were constructed for internal use.

QUESTION 5

For how many years has your company been capitalizing software costs?

Responses indicate that the vast majority of the companies in this study have been capitalizing software for six years or less. This response might be interpreted to mean that there is a trend toward the capitalization of software costs. However, it should be kept in mind that many software companies have not been in existence for more than six years.

QUESTION 6

Software costs that are not expensed are capitalized because _____.

The most frequently given reasons for capitalizing software costs are that either an asset has been created or the matching concept requires that costs be matched to the period of expected benefit.

QUESTION 7

Software costs that are not capitalized are expensed because _____.

The most frequently given reasons for expensing software costs are that such costs are either research and development or there is uncertainty as to realization.

QUESTION 8

If a product intended for sale is found to be unmarketable but the coding is partially or wholly reusable, and is reused in a new product intended for sale, how are the coding costs allocated?

Responses to this question reveal that the vast majority of companies (75 percent) allocate the coding costs of a product failure to that product even though the code may later be used in another product.

QUESTION 9

How are development costs shared between an internally used product and a product developed for sale that uses all or a substantial portion of the code?

Software construction costs that are incurred for a program that is both used internally and sold are generally allocated exclusively to the product intended for sale.

QUESTION 10

Does your company provide reserves for future maintenance costs incurred in fulfilling warranty obligations?

The vast majority of companies (76 percent) do not provide reserves for future maintenance costs incurred in fulfilling warranty obligations. In cases where reserves were estimated, the estimation methods used included:

1. Prior year history.
2. Percentage of revenue.
3. Future expected returns for failure within warranty period.
4. Past experience plus previous 90 days sales.
5. Estimated labor hours to be expended.
6. Project by project basis.
7. Proration of revenues plus specific cost evaluation.
8. Pure guess—new company with no previous history.
9. Deferral of recognition of maintenance revenue rather than establishment of a reserve for future maintenance costs.

QUESTION 11

Do you think the accounting treatment for purchased software should be different than the accounting treatment for comparable internally developed software?

A clear majority of respondents (56 percent) do not think that the accounting treatment for purchased software should be different than that for internally constructed software. For those respondents indicating that there should be different accounting treatment, the main reasons given were:

1. Costs associated with internally developed software are not as easily identified and are subject to judgment rather than unequivocal evidence.
2. Specific costs are more readily identified for purchased software and its specific use/life can be matched to product sales.
3. Purchased software has a predetermined value (purchase price) and should be an asset, whereas internally constructed software is ever-changing and is a period expense.
4. It is too difficult to allocate costs and resources and to identify costs associated with software construction. Capitalizing internally constructed software opens the door to manipulation of income by over-allocating costs to capitalized software.
5. Purchased software has an established market value, whereas internally constructed software costs are at risk.
6. Purchased software products have generally passed technical marketability and user testing prior to purchase. Future use and benefit are much more likely than for constructed software.
7. It is extremely difficult to separate R&D expenses for internally constructed software.
8. Purchased software is generally a standard product, whereas internally constructed software is custom.

QUESTION 12

The inability to include software costs on the balance sheet adversely affects your ability to raise capital.

The views of the private and public companies regarding the effect of software accounting policy on the ability to raise capital are summarized in this question.

A slight majority of private companies disagreed with the statement. However, the public companies disagreed with the statement by a margin of 4 to 1.

For those respondents who agreed with the statement, some of the reasons given were:

1. Companies that expense software construction costs are placed in an inferior position to those which capitalize such costs, especially in start-up situations.
2. Income producing assets need to be reflected on the balance sheet in order to fairly present the valuation of the company. A company would be grossly undervalued if these costs were expensed immediately.
3. Banks treat financial statements very literally.
4. Expensing software costs adversely affects current earnings.
5. Privately owned companies and companies that are not a subsidiary of a major conglomerate are at a definite disadvantage if they expense software costs.

Those who disagreed did so for the following reasons:

1. Ability to raise capital is impacted by future revenues from software development rather than the current balance sheet. Expensing software construction costs actually improves future profitability.
2. Other indicia of financial strength and leverage (for example, revenue projections and business plan) are more meaningful than software accounting policy.
3. The amounts involved are not material (but, see comments to Question 3).
4. The investment community offers a different multiple to companies that capitalize software. Bankers tend to delete software from the balance sheet.
5. The ability to raise capital is a function of profit and loss and growth experience. (But how is profit and loss affected by a firm's software accounting policy?)
6. The majority of assets on many vendor company balance sheets consists of cash and receivables.
7. The market is sophisticated enough to know the software business. Providers of capital to the software industry recognize special situations.
8. The cost of software on a balance sheet usually has no relationship to its value.

QUESTION 13

The inability to include software costs on the balance sheet adversely affects the interest rate your company must pay to obtain capital.

The vast majority of both private and public companies do not think the interest rate they must pay on borrowed capital is adversely affected by the inability to include software costs on the balance sheet.

QUESTION 14

If all software development costs were expensed rather than capitalized the level of these expenditures for software companies would have to be much lower; companies would be forced to put a cap on investment in new product programs in order to reflect good earnings performance to shareholders.

The view of private and public companies on the relationship of software accounting policy on investment and growth is summarized. A small majority of private companies (51.4 percent) feel that investment and growth would be inhibited by requiring software construction costs to be expensed rather than capitalized. A substantial minority of public companies (33.3 percent) feel the same way. Overall, the sample firms are about evenly divided on the issue, with 40.7 percent agreeing, 43.0 percent disagreeing, and 16.3 percent having no opinion.

QUESTION 15

If all software development costs were expensed rather than capitalized, the price of your company's stock, if publicly traded, would be adversely affected.

Private companies are about evenly split on this question. Public companies disagree by a two-to-one margin. Overall, a majority of companies (56.8 percent) disagrees that expensing software adversely affects stock price.

QUESTION 16

If all software development costs were expensed rather than capitalized, your company's long-term growth would be adversely affected.

The vast majority of both private and public firms do not think that expensing software construction costs adversely affects long-term growth. Private and public companies disagreed with the statement by ratios of two to one and five to one, respectively, which is even greater than the disagreement rate for Question 14, which asked basically the same question. On the other hand, a substantial minority of private firms (32.4 percent) do think that expensing software construction costs adversely affects long-term growth.

QUESTION 17

Your company sometimes purchases software that could be internally developed because it is easier to justify placing purchased software costs on the balance sheet.

This question was included because it was discovered, during the course of the interviews, that some companies choose the method of obtaining software based on its effect on the balance sheet and income statement. There is sometimes a tendency to classify software as an asset in order to avoid placing software costs in the income statement, and there is widespread feeling that costs expended for the purchase of software are easier to justify for asset treatment than are costs for the construction of software. (See Questions 6 and 7.) Some firms, it is argued, resort to the R&D partnership vehicle in order to capitalize costs that would otherwise be expensed as software construction costs.

Almost 90 percent of the companies included in the survey disagree with the view that a company will purchase software rather than construct it in order to justify its inclusion in the balance sheet.

QUESTION 18

If company policy were to expense all software costs as incurred rather than to capitalize a portion of software costs, my company's net income would be reduced by _____ percent.

The vast majority of private (69.4 percent) and public companies (84.3 percent) would have a less than 5 percent reduction in net income if software costs that are not being capitalized would have been expensed instead. However, this fact does not mean that software expenditures are immaterial for the vast majority of software vendor companies, because many firms are presently expensing rather than capitalizing most or all of their software costs anyway. Even if this factor is taken into consideration, 30.6 percent of private companies and 15.7 percent of public companies would have a reduction in net income of at least 5 percent, which may be considered a material reduction. If materiality is defined as a 10 percent reduction in net income, then the percentages for private and public companies would be 22.2 percent and 15.7 percent, respectively. It is safe to say that software expenditures as a percentage of net sales is significant for all software vendors, as such costs are among the major costs incurred by a software vendor.

QUESTION 19

Has your company ever used an R&D partnership, limited partnership or other off balance sheet arrangement in connection with software development? If yes, what were your reasons for using such an arrangement?

More than 90 percent of the firms included in the survey did not use R&D partnerships or other off balance sheet arrangements in connection with software development expenditures.

The main reasons given for answering "yes" were either to boost earnings or to spread risks and obtain favorable financing terms. Five of the six companies using off balance sheet financing are publicly held.

QUESTION 20

On which categories of software is the investment tax credit or R&D tax credit taken?

This question asked: "On which categories of software is the investment tax credit or R&D tax credit taken?" A nonresponse might be due to the fact that: (1) the tax credit was not taken, (2) the company filling out the questionnaire did not incur all four categories of software costs, or (3) the person filling out the questionnaire did not know the answer and the tax manager was out of town. The computed percentages used 88 as a denominator, the number of companies that completed the questionnaire. The percentages are conservatively stated because of the limiting factors mentioned above.

The most frequently taken credit was the R&D tax credit, for internally constructed software intended for sale, which was taken by at least 72.7 percent of the companies surveyed. The reason why more companies did not take advantage of the available tax credits is not known, although it should be mentioned that many software expenditures do not qualify for either tax credit.[2]

QUESTION 21

Is the same software item ever: Capitalized for tax purposes and expensed for financial statement purposes? Capitalized for financial statement purposes and expensed for tax purposes?

While the vast majority of companies treat the same software item the same way for both financial and tax purposes, a significant minority have different treatments in some cases. Many firms did not respond to this question. Perhaps the high nonresponse rate is because many firms expense all software for both tax and financial reporting purposes.

QUESTION 22

If software is capitalized for both financial statement and tax purposes, are the amortization method and time period used the same?

The vast majority of firms that capitalize software for both financial statement and tax purposes use the same amortization method and time period. However, for a significant minority of firms, there are different treatments. Many firms did not respond to this question, presumably, because they expense all software costs.

QUESTION 23

How is software classified?

The majority of companies classify software as intangible for both federal and state tax purposes, although for a significant minority of companies it may be tangible. The tax treatment for sales, use, and property tax is determined on a state by state basis, so it is possible that a software firm may have a software item taxed as tangible personal property in one state, but have an identical item exempt from tax if sold in another state, because that state classifies it as intangible. In some states, software sold in the form of a magnetic tape or disk is taxed as tangible, whereas the same software, if delivered over telephone wires or by satellite, would be intangible and exempt from tax. In some states, custom software is exempt from tax, whereas "canned" or "off-the-shelf" software is taxable.

QUESTION 24

Has your company been a party to litigation involving the sales taxability of software in the last three years?

More than 90 percent of the firms responding to this question have not been involved in software sales tax litigation in the last three years. Of the seven companies that have been parties to litigation (eight companies checked the "yes" box—one nonlitigant is assisting in the litigation efforts of others), at least five cases involve California.

QUESTION 25

Which public accounting firm signs the opinion for your company's financial statements?

Price Waterhouse audits more publicly held companies than any of the other firms, followed closely by Ernst & Whinney. Of the "big 8" firms, Touche Ross & Co. audits the fewest public firms.

Arthur Andersen & Co. heads the list for private firms, followed closely by Arthur Young & Co. Overall, Price Waterhouse audited the most companies, followed by Ernst & Whinney.

QUESTION 26

Total software related revenues for the most recent fiscal year were _____.

More than 72 percent of the sample was drawn from companies having annual software-related revenues of $20 million or less. Sixteen percent, or 14 companies, had software related revenues of more than $50 million. As expected, private firms generally have less sales than public companies, but two of the private firms had sales in excess of $50 million, which would rank them in the top quarter of publicly held software companies.

QUESTION 27

Is the company privately or publicly held?

Fifty-one of the firms (58 percent) were publicly held. The other 37 (42 percent) were privately held.

This sample was heavily weighted in favor of publicly held firms. Although there are approximately 4,000 privately held software companies and less than 100 publicly held software firms, the majority of respondents were publicly held. This response is due to the sample selection method chosen. All publicly held software firms that could be identified were sent a questionnaire. Only a relatively small percentage of privately held software firms received a questionnaire, and these firms were chosen on the basis of sales volume.

CHAPTER 4

Software-User Accounting Policies and Practices

Introduction

This chapter presents a survey of the accounting policies of 65 software-user companies. As in Chapter 2, the information is in tabular form with the companies listed alphabetically.

The data were obtained from examining the financial statement footnotes of 4,197 companies for fiscal 1981–82 and 3,104 companies for fiscal 1982–83, using NAARS. Robert Kueppers of Deloitte Haskins & Sells, New York, provided the author with access to the NAARS data base.

Survey of Software Accounting Policies—Software User Companies

Company	Policy	Annual Report Date	Auditor
1. AMDAHL CORPORATION	Engineering and development costs are expensed as incurred. The company anticipates that continued engineering and development efforts will be required to maintain and improve the efficiency of its high-technology products and to develop new products.	December 25, 1981	Arthur Andersen & Company
2. AMERICAN MANAGEMENT SYSTEMS, INC.	Revenue from sales of "off-the-shelf" software packages is recorded at the time of contract signing, less an amount approximately equal to costs required to complete the performance of the contract which is later recognized on a percentage of completion basis. Revenues from cost-shared software research and development contracts are recorded using the percentage of completion method. In 1982, when such cost-shared work began, the company recorded approximately $778,000 of revenues relating to cost-shared research and development projects. Revenues for computer services are recorded on the basis of usage at scheduled contract prices per unit of production, or the contract minimum monthly charge, whichever is greater. Fixed assets and purchased computer software and software licenses are recorded at cost. Software and software licenses are generally amortized over five years using the straight-line method.	December 31, 1982	Price Waterhouse & Company
3. APPLIED DEVICES CORPORATION	Sales relating to certain long-term contracts, some of which contain provision for incentive fees and penalties, are recorded in the accounts principally under the percentage-of-completion method. Revenue, under certain contracts calling for both the development of software and the production of hardware, is recognized on the percentage-of-completion	October 31, 1982	Coopers & Lybrand

Survey of Software Accounting Policies—Software User Companies (continued)

Company	Policy	Annual Report Date	Auditor
4. BANK SOUTH CORPORATION	method for the software development phase of the contract and on a unit-delivery basis for the remainder of the contract. Under the percentage-of-completion method, revenue is based on that percentage of the contract price costs incurred to date bear to total estimated costs. Where changes in contract cost estimates result in adjustments, the full income effect of such adjustments is recognized in the accounting period in which the change is made. Provision is made for the total loss anticipated where the estimate of total contract costs indicates a loss. The effect of overhead rate adjustments resulting from government audits is recorded in the year the rates are finalized, and notification is received by the company. Costs of computer software purchased from vendors are deferred and amortized over their estimated useful lives.	December 31, 1982	Ernst & Whinney
5. BISCAYNE FEDERAL SAVINGS AND LOAN ASSOCIATION	Costs incurred for acquisition or development of computer software are capitalized in other assets and amortized over five years.	June 30, 1982	Deloitte Haskins & Sells
6. CGA COMPUTER ASSOCIATES, INC.	Revenue consulting services, performed principally on a time and material basis, is recognized as the work is performed, at agreed upon billing rates. Revenue from proprietary software products which are marketed to customers primarily under annual and perpetual license arrangements is recognized at the time the product is installed and unconditionally accepted by the customer. As a result of the amortization of software packages and goodwill and the related tax effect, net income under the pooling-of-	April 30, 1982	Price Waterhouse & Company

7. CADO SYSTEMS CORPORATION	interests method of accounting would exceed the purchase method of accounting by approximately $2,700,000 per year over the five year amortization period. The application of the purchase method of accounting to the ASC combination results in the recording of software packages and goodwill. The fair value of software packages, $11,770,000, which is based upon an independent appraisal, and goodwill in the amount of $6,562,000, are being amortized on a straight-line basis over their estimated useful lives, a five-year period. Computer software programs acquired by the company are capitalized and amortized by use of the straight-line method over their expected useful lives—generally three years.	December 31, 1981	Peat, Marwick, Mitchell & Company
8. CHITTENDEN CORPORATION	Provision for depreciation and amortization is computed by the straight-line method for financial statement purposes based on the estimated useful lives of the respective assets and accelerated methods for income tax purposes. The difference between book and tax depreciation is reflected as a timing difference in the tax provision. The estimated life of software for book purposes is five years.	December 31, 1981	R. F. Lavigne & Company
9. COMMERCE CLEARING HOUSE, INC.	Purchased computer software is amortized over five years.	December 31, 1982	Touche Ross & Company
10. COMPUTER NETWORK CORPORATION	Internal software development costs are expensed as incurred, whereas software purchased is capitalized and amortized over estimated useful lives. Capitalized software is currently being amortized over a five-year period.	March 31, 1982	Arthur Andersen & Company
11. COMPUTER-VISION CORPORATION	The company expenses all research and product and software development costs as incurred.	December 31, 1981	Price Waterhouse & Company

Survey of Software Accounting Policies—Software User Companies (continued)

Company	Policy	Annual Report Date	Auditor
12. CORADIAN CORPORATION	Certain internal software development costs related to the new management information system have been capitalized.	December 31, 1981	Peat, Marwick, Mitchell & Company
13. DENELCOR, INC.	The costs and expenses related to basic research and development are expensed as incurred. Costs of software development are also expensed as incurred, until such time as the remaining costs, if any, are realizable through future production and sale. Software development costs capitalized are amortized using the straight-line method based upon the asset's estimated useful life.	December 31, 1982	Arthur Andersen & Company
14. DIMIS, INC.	Service revenues result from the company's software maintenance and development contracts and system rental contracts and are recognized as earned over the contract periods.	December 31, 1981	Peat, Marwick, Mitchell & Company
15. DOCUTEL CORPORATION	Amortization of purchased software is provided by the straight-line method over the expected period to be benefited of five years.	December 31, 1981	Arthur Young & Company
16. THE DUN AND BRADSTREET CORPORATION	Purchased computer software ($21,625,000) is amortized over five to seven years using the straight-line method.	December 31, 1982	Coopers & Lybrand
17. DURR-FILLAUER MEDICAL, INC.	The company charges to expense all research and development costs as incurred. These costs are related to computer software development. The total costs charged to expense in 1982, 1981, and 1980 were $160,000, $84,000, and $59,000, respectively.	December 31, 1982	Wilson, Price, Barranco & Billingsley
18. ELECTRONIC DATA SYSTEMS CORPORATION	Purchased software is being amortized on a straight-line basis over a five-year life or life of the related customer contract, whichever is less.	June 30, 1982	Arthur Young & Company

19. ENSOURCE, INC.	Other property primarily consists of furniture and fixtures, leasehold improvements, and computer software that are being depreciated or amortized on a declining balance method using useful lives of three to five years.	December 31, 1982	Arthur Andersen & Company
20. EUROPEAN AMERICAN BANKCORP	Deferred charges consist of certain software development costs relating to significant system modifications. Amortization is computed on a straight-line basis over a three year period commencing upon implementation of these system modifications.	December 31, 1982	Peat, Marwick, Mitchell & Company
21. FIRST EMPIRE STATE CORPORATION	Other assets include deferred software costs related to the development of major computer systems for administrative purposes. Such costs are amortized on the straight-line method over three to five years—the estimated useful lives of the assets.	December 31, 1981	Peat, Marwick, Mitchell & Company
22. FIRST KENTUCKY NATIONAL CORPORATION	Purchased software costs and other direct costs associated with the development of operating and management information systems are capitalized and amortized by the straight-line method over periods not exceeding seven years from the time such systems become operational. Systems modifications and maintenance costs are expensed as incurred.	December 31, 1982	Coopers & Lybrand
23. HI-G INCORPORATED	Software costs of $546,000 and $396,000 are being amortized for 1982 and 1981, respectively, over five years.	April 3, 1982	Laventhol & Horwath
24. IMS INTERNATIONAL, INC.	Costs of developing and implementing new or improved computer systems are capitalized over two to five year periods.	December 31, 1982	Arthur Andersen & Company
25. ISC SYSTEMS CORPORATION	Revenue Recognition. The company manufactures and sells on-line teller terminal systems used in the financial industry. The system includes hardware, general operating system software and custom application software. Revenue is recognized upon acceptance and delivery of the system. In those cases where the hardware is delivered prior to the acceptance of the	June 24, 1982	Deloitte Haskins & Sells

Survey of Software Accounting Policies—Software User Companies (continued)

Company	Policy	Annual Report Date	Auditor
	system, no revenue is recognized until such acceptance is completed. Service and other revenues are recognized over the contractual period or as the services are provided. Research and Development Costs. All research, product development, software development, and engineering costs are charged to expense as incurred.		
26. ITT	Computer Software Costs. Costs of development and implementation of computer software not directly related to research and development are capitalized and included in Other Assets. These costs are amortized over the lesser of five years or their useful life.	December 31, 1982	Arthur Andersen & Company
27. ITT— INSURANCE AND FINANCE SUBSIDIARY	Costs of development and implementation of computer software are capitalized and included in "Other Assets." These costs are amortized over the lesser of five years or their useful life. As of December 31, 1982 and 1981, these costs amounted to $27,914,000 and $4,315,000, net of amortization.	December 31, 1982	Arthur Andersen & Company
28. INTERGRAPH CORPORATION	Revenues on product sales and software are recognized as equipment and software are shipped under the contract. A certain portion of revenue from systems sales is not recognized until installation is complete and the warranty period has expired. Billings, which are made at specified times during the performance of the contract or agreement, generally do not coincide with the recognition of revenue. Income from cost-plus-fee contracts is recognized as costs are incurred and fees are earned under the contract. Income from maintenance and operating lease contracts is recognized monthly over the life of the contract.	December 31, 1982	Ernst & Whinney
29. KAY CORPORATION	Computer system and software costs, included in other assets, are capitalized and amortized on a straight-line basis over three years.	December 31, 1982	Arthur Young & Company

30. THE L. E. MYERS COMPANY	On February 22, 1980, Myers acquired Scott & Scott Consultants, Inc., which develops computer software systems for electric utilities. The acquisition was accounted for as a purchase and results of operations are included since acquisition. Intangibles in the amount of $203,000 were recognized in the acquisition and are being amortized over a three year period using the straight-line method.	December 31, 1982	Main Hurdman
31. LIFEMARK CORPORATION	Computer software development and installation costs are deferred and amortized on a straight-line basis over the useful lives of the applications not in excess of five years.	December 31, 1981	Peat, Marwick, Mitchell & Company
32. LINCOLN INCOME LIFE INSURANCE COMPANY	Computer software is depreciated over five years using the straight-line method.	December 31, 1982	Christen, Brown & Rufer
33. MAGNUSON COMPUTER SYSTEMS, INC.	The company operates in one industry segment which includes the design, development, manufacturing, marketing, and servicing of general purpose computer systems which are designed to operate with software and peripheral equipment offered by or compatible with that of IBM. Revenue Recognition. Accounting Change. The policy for the recognition of revenue was changed in the fourth quarter of 1981. The new policy results in revenue recognition at time of product installation for those transactions where the company has installation responsibility. During 1980 and 1979, revenue was recognized on such transactions at time of shipment. This change was made because significantly longer periods of time were experienced in 1981 between shipment and installation. No change was made to the policy where the company does not have installation responsibility or to the requirement that the company have a firm order and that financing arrangements have been completed.	December 31, 1981	Deloitte Haskins & Sells

71

Survey of Software Accounting Policies—Software User Companies *(continued)*

Company	Policy	Annual Report Date	Auditor
34. MANAGEMENT ASSISTANCE, INC.	The new revenue recognition accounting policy adopted in 1981 has been applied retroactively to the beginning of the year and the cumulative effect of the change on prior years ($1,017,000) is included in the 1981 results of operations. Application of the new accounting policy during 1981 increased loss before cumulative effect of accounting change by $1,066,000 ($.22 per share). The total impact increased the 1981 net loss by $2,083,000.	September 30, 1982	Peat, Marwick, Mitchell & Company
35. MATHEMATICAL APPLICATIONS GROUP, INC.	Research and development costs are charged to expense when incurred and include engineering and product enhancement costs.	March 31, 1982	Ernst & Whinney
	Research and Development. Research and development costs (principally software and systems development costs) are charged to expense when incurred. Such costs amounted to approximately $1,183,000 (1982), $1,138,000 (1981), and $829,000 (1980).		
36. MAY ENERGY PARTNERS, LTD.	Computer software was implemented to maintain May Energy's tax accounts and to prepare its tax reports. Such costs are being amortized over five years using the straight-line method.	December 31, 1982	Arthur Andersen & Company
37. METPATH, INC.	Computer software development and installation costs (unamortized balance of $1,311,000 in 1981 and $358,000 in 1980) are deferred and will be amortized on a straight-line basis over periods of four to five years.	September 30, 1981	Laventhol & Horwath
38. MOBILE COMMUNICATIONS CORPORATION OF AMERICA	Other assets consist primarily of debenture issuance costs, organizational costs, and data processing software cost. These costs are being amortized over periods ranging from 5 to 40 years.	December 31, 1982	Arthur Andersen & Company

39. MODULAR COMPUTER SYSTEMS, INC.	Amortization of Other Assets. The costs of purchased computer technology are amortized on a straight-line method over the estimated development period. Costs of purchased software and licenses are amortized on straight-line and unit-of-sale methods, respectively, over the estimated product lives. Costs of management information systems are amortized on a straight-line method over the estimated period of benefit.	December 31, 1982	Price Waterhouse & Company
40. MULTIVEST, INC.	Depreciation and amortization, computed by the straight-line method for financial statement purposes, are provided over the useful lives of the various classes of property and equipment. Intangible assets, primarily software costs, are being amortized over their respective lives. During 1981, the company revised earlier estimates of the useful lives for calculating depreciation of all computer hardware and software. This change in accounting estimate had the effect of increasing the 1981 net loss by $316,000 ($.51 per share).	December 31, 1982	Coopers & Lybrand
41. MUNFORD, INC.	Software development costs are capitalized and amortized over five years using the straight-line method.	December 30, 1982	Touche Ross & Company
42. NATIONAL CITY CORPORATION	Costs of major new software are capitalized and amortized over a period not exceeding five years.	December 31, 1982	Ernst & Whinney
43. NATIONAL DATA COMMUNICATIONS, INCORPORATED	Programming fees are recognized based on hourly rates as the work is performed. Software license fees are recognized based on the respective contract terms which vary significantly. The company currently either grants a 75 percent partially paid-up software license with continuing monthly license fees for the remaining 25 percent or grants a license on a rental basis with no initial fee but continuing monthly fees. Equipment sales are recognized when the equipment has been tested in the company's offices and shipped to the hospital for installation.	October 31, 1981	Peat, Marwick, Mitchell & Company

Survey of Software Accounting Policies—Software User Companies (continued)

Company	Policy	Annual Report Date	Auditor
44. PBA, INC.	Maintenance and computer operations fees are recognized on a monthly basis in accordance with contract terms with related costs recognized as incurred.	June 30, 1982	Richard A. Eisner & Company
45. PACIFIC STANDARD LIFE COMPANY	Capitalized computer software costs (which include $40,000 of capitalized interest) will be amortized using the straight-line method over five years. Such amortization will begin during fiscal 1983, when the software will be operational.	December 31, 1982	Coopers & Lybrand
46. QUALITY CARE, INC.	Deferrable computer software costs have been capitalized and are being amortized over 5 and 20 year periods.	November 30, 1981	Touche Ross & Company
47. RAYMOND INTER-NATIONAL INCOR-PORATED	Start-up costs incurred in connection with branch office operations and computer software costs related to the installation of new equipment and to the development of new programs have been deferred and are being amortized on a straight-line basis over periods not exceeding 36 months. Acquired computer software is being amortized over six years on a straight-line basis.	December 31, 1981	Price Waterhouse & Company
48. THE REYNOLDS AND REYNOLDS COMPANY	Software license fees are charged for the use of company-developed computer programs (such as accounting and inventory control) by customers who either purchase or lease in-house computer equipment. These revenues are recognized over the term of the support agreement which is generally five to seven years.	September 30, 1982	Deloitte Haskins & Sells

74

49. SEI CORPORATION	Property and equipment are stated at cost. Depreciation and amortization are provided using the straight-line method for financial reporting purposes, while accelerated methods are used for tax purposes. Estimated useful lives for purchased software are five to eight years.	December 31, 1982	Arthur Andersen & Company
50. SEIBELS BRUCE GROUP, INC.	Initial license charges from computer software systems are recognized at the time of the contractual agreement. Monthly license charges from computer software systems and income from services are recognized as billed and earned. Systems research and development costs are expensed as incurred. Such costs were $11,875,000 in 1982 ($6,763,000 in 1981 and $4,441,000 in 1980).	December 31, 1982	Clarkson, Harden and Gantt
51. SHARED MEDICAL SYSTEMS CORPORATION	Property and equipment are stated at cost. Depreciation and amortization are provided using the straight-line method over the estimated useful lives. The cost of purchased software is capitalized and amortized over a five year period while the cost of in-house developed software is expensed as incurred. The company expenses research and development costs in the year in which they are incurred. These expenses are primarily computer costs and salaries to enhance and develop applications. These expenses amounted to $13,724,000 in 1982, $10,551,000 in 1981, and $8,205,000 in 1980.	December 31, 1982	Arthur Andersen & Company
52. THE STATESMAN GROUP, INC.	Property and Equipment. Property and equipment, which includes data software costs, are reported at cost, less accumulated depreciation. Provisions for depreciation are computed by straight-line and declining-balance methods. Data software costs, which consist of payments of outside parties, are being amortized over five years. The unamortized balance of data software costs at December 31, 1982 is $2,072,000.	December 31, 1982	Ernst & Whinney

Survey of Software Accounting Policies—Software User Companies (concluded)

Company	Policy	Annual Report Date	Auditor
53. SYNTECH INTERNATIONAL	The cost of a software distribution license, obtained in exchange for cancellation of a trade note receivable, is being amortized over two years. At December 31, 1982, the unamortized cost related to such license included in other assets approximated $88,000.	December 31, 1982	Deloitte Haskins & Sells
54. TECHTRAN INDUSTRIES, INC.	The cost of acquired computer software and product design is being amortized over three years on the straight-line method.	August 31, 1981	Cortland L. Brovitz & Company
55. TERADYNE, INC.	The company's products are highly technical in nature and require a large and continuing engineering and development effort. Purchased computer software is amortized over its expected useful life of five years. All other engineering and developmental costs are expensed as incurred.	December 31, 1982	Coopers & Lybrand
56. TYMSHARE, INC.	The cost of software developed by the company is charged to expense as incurred. Purchased software is capitalized and amortized over its estimated life.	December 31, 1982	Arthur Andersen & Company
57. THE UNION METAL MANUFACTURING COMPANY	Software costs are recorded at cost less amortization computed on the straight-line method over the estimated useful life of 15 years.	December 31, 1982	Ernst & Whinney
58. UNITED STATES MUTUAL REAL ESTATE INVESTMENT TRUST	Computer equipment and software are stated at cost less accumulated depreciation and amortization. Depreciation and amortization are charged to operations under the straight-line method over the estimated useful lives of the assets which range from five to ten years.	April 30, 1982	Price Waterhouse & Company

59. U. S. SHELTER	Internally developed computer software costs of $325,000 in 1982 and $206,000 in 1981, expected to benefit future periods by improving management information systems and reducing accounting costs, are being deferred and amortized over four years.	December 31, 1982	Ernst & Whinney
60. UNITED TELECOM-MUNICATIONS	Software sales are recorded on a percentage-of-completion basis.	December 31, 1982	Arthur Young & Company
61. WALLACE COMPUTER SERVICES, INC.	Purchase costs of computer software are amortized over their estimated useful lives. Internal development costs are expensed.	July 31, 1982	Arthur Andersen & Company
62. WASHINGTON NATIONAL CORPORATION	Certain costs in developing computer software are deferred when incurred and amortized on a straight-line basis over 10 years or less.	December 31, 1982	Ernst & Whinney
63. WHITTAKER CORPORATION	Purchased software is related to the medical information systems business and is amortized using the straight-line method over seven years.	October 31, 1982	Ernst & Whinney
64. WYLE LABORA-TORIES	The cost of purchased software is being amortized principally over seven years using the straight-line method.	January 31, 1982	Arthur Andersen & Company
65. ZALE CORPORATION	Computer software costs related to the development of major systems are capitalized as incurred and amortized over their useful lives using the straight-line method.	March 31, 1983	Arthur Andersen & Company

CHAPTER 5

Survey of Software Users

Introduction

This chapter summarizes the mail questionnaire responses that were received from 216 software user companies.[1]

QUESTION 1

What amortization method and time period range are used for financial statement purposes to amortize: (1) purchased/leased: (*a*) systems software, (*b*) applications software; (2) internally developed: (*a*) systems software, (*b*) applications software?

Two companies in three (66.7 percent) capitalize purchased systems software and about the same percentage (62.0 percent) capitalize purchased applications software. The number of firms that capitalize internally constructed systems and applications software is much lower, 10.6 percent and 11.6 percent, respectively. For those companies that capitalize software, about 90 percent use the straight-line method of amortization. Furthermore, about 90 percent of capitalized software costs are amortized over five years or less.

Some companies gave multiple responses to Question 1. Others did not respond to some portions of the question. A few companies mentioned that software costing less than some threshold amount is expensed, and software costing more than that amount is capitalized. The threshold amounts mentioned ranged from $20,000 to $2 million. Several companies amortize systems software over the life of the hardware. A few amortize software that is "bundled" with the hardware and expense software that is not.

QUESTION 2

What costs are capitalized for internally developed software?

As was true of software vendors, the categories of internally constructed software cost of software users that tend to be capitalized most frequently are design, coding, and testing costs.

QUESTION 3

For compilers, system control programs, and other software that is an integral part of the hardware, the software is _____.

For compilers, system control programs, and other software that is an integral part of the hardware, the software is most often amortized over the same period as the hardware (50.0 percent) or expensed (36.1 percent). A few (6.6 percent) use a shorter period. The remainder (7.2 percent) amortize over three to five years or over the lease term.

QUESTION 4

Software maintenance and enhancement costs are _____.

The vast majority of companies expense maintenance (94.9 percent) and enhancement costs (83.8 percent) as incurred.

QUESTION 5

During the amortization period, are there periodic financial reviews or checkpoints to determine the need for write-offs of assets?

Five eighths of the firms responding to this question have periodic financial reviews or checkpoints during the amortization period to determine the need for a write-off of assets. Many firms did not respond to this question, because they expense rather than capitalize software costs.

QUESTION 6

Software costs appearing on the balance sheet represent what percent of total assets?

Virtually all of the companies surveyed have negligible software costs appearing on the balance sheet. If materiality is defined as 5 percent of total assets, then only three companies out of 216 (1.4 percent) have a material amount of software costs on the balance sheet. If materiality is 10 percent of total assets, then only one company (0.5 percent) has a material amount of software costs. That company reported software assets totaling 20 percent of total assets.

QUESTION 7

Software costs that are not expensed are capitalized because _____.

The two most frequently mentioned reasons for capitalizing software are because of the matching concept and the belief that an asset has been created. Other reasons included:

1. Enhancement of net income, earnings per share, and ability to raise capital.
2. Software is accounted for in the same manner as hardware because of bundling or otherwise.
3. Compatibility with tax treatment; IRS requires it.
4. Purchased software costs are readily identifiable.
5. The licensing agreement spans more than one accounting period.

QUESTION 8

Software costs that are not capitalized are expensed because _____.

The most frequently given reasons for expensing rather than capitalizing software are:

1. Uncertainty as to realization makes expensing prudent.
2. They are immaterial in amount.
3. They are expensed for tax purposes, and we want to use the same accounting method per tax and book whenever possible.
4. Such costs are considered research and development.
5. R&D cost elements are not easily separated from non-R&D costs, so all costs are expensed.
6. Our CPA firm strongly recommends that such costs be expensed. Management is of the opinion that certain software costs should be capitalized.

Other reasons include:

1. Software maintenance costs are period costs.
2. The realization period is short.
3. Expensing is conservative.
4. Software is a cost of doing business.
5. The ongoing expense would be about equal to the amortization.
6. It is difficult to measure the cost of internally constructed software, so it is expensed.
7. Costs incurred subsequent to the implementation of the system that do not extend its useful life are expensed.
8. Useful life is difficult to estimate, so software costs are expensed.

QUESTION 9

How are software costs reflected on the balance sheet?

About one company in three does not include purchased systems software (36.8 percent) or purchased applications software (36.7 percent) on the balance sheet. For those companies that do include purchased software on the balance sheet, it is most often included in fixed assets, with other noncurrent assets as the second choice.

More than four companies out of five do not include internally constructed systems software (83.2 percent) or applications software (82.1 percent) on the balance sheet. For those that do, the most frequent inclusions are either as other noncurrent assets or as fixed assets.

QUESTION 10

If software is leased, are the accounting rules for capital leasing considered when determining how to account for the software cost?

For leased software, the majority of companies (57.4 percent) consider the accounting rules for capital leasing either a matter of corporate policy (41.4 percent) or in cases where the cost is more than a certain dollar amount (16.0 percent). For those companies that responded "other," the most frequently given comments were:

1. We don't lease software; not applicable.
2. None are of a capital nature.
3. Only if tied to leased hardware.

QUESTION 11

Do you think the accounting treatment for purchased software should be different than the accounting treatment for comparable internally developed software?

When asked whether the accounting treatment for purchased software should be different than the accounting treatment for comparable internally constructed software, the majority of software users (56.7 percent) said no, which corresponds closely with the percentage of software vendors (56.2 percent) no responses. About 3 companies in 10 (30.9 percent) felt that the accounting treatments should be different. The most frequently given reasons for both choices are listed below.

SAME TREATMENT

1. The utility of the software, whether purchased or constructed internally is the same. They both provide the same result. The method of acquisition should not dictate accounting treatment.

2. An asset is created whether it is purchased or constructed internally.
3. If comparable software exists, it may still be of economic benefit to construct the software internally. Why penalize a company by requiring a different accounting treatment?
4. If comparable software exists, internally constructed software probably is not a R&D effort.
5. Leads to skewed decisions for make/buy analysis when user has budget constraints. Implies internally constructed software is substantially uncertain as to success of effort, which is not consistent with business assumptions in project authorization.
6. Consistency.
7. Software is software.
8. All software should be expensed at time of purchase or as internally constructed.
9. The decision to capitalize any costs should be based on whether the costs represent a bona fide asset and meet a recoverability test.
10. The matching principle would require that costs be associated with benefits regardless of how procured.

DIFFERENT TREATMENT

1. Purchased software has a fixed-life payout evaluation. Internally constructed software is related to basic operations without a finite cost or benefit.
2. As a practical matter, a determination between system development costs and ongoing system utilization and R&D costs is not worthwhile to split out for the amounts involved.
3. Expensing internally constructed software provides a legitimate means to reduce taxable income as well as the tax liability.
4. The cost of purchased software is readily determinable. It is more difficult to measure the cost of internally constructed software.
5. Guidelines need to be developed to address the control and maintenance of internally constructed software.
6. Internally constructed software is an R&D expenditure.
7. Differences in matching costs and benefits.
8. The record-keeping necessary for internally constructed software would be extensive and probably not adhered to.
9. Internal costs for constructing software (salaries of systems personnel) are part of the ongoing costs of the systems department.
10. The effort required to identify cost for internally constructed software exceeds the value to the financial statements obtained by capitalization.

11. Because of the subjectivity involved, capitalization of the costs of internally constructed software could lead to abuses in order to improve reported net income.
12. Purchased software, to be saleable, must demonstrate its utility through numerous successful implementations. Internally constructed software is inherently more risky, and consequently, the prospects of asset realization are much less certain.
13. Purchased software has a one-time cost. Internally constructed software has several costs involved—such as salaries, supplies, and computer time—for an undetermined amount of time. The expense of the internal software should be recognized over the period of time it took to construct it.
14. Internally constructed software costs are mainly personnel costs. Personnel costs are not capitalized unless they become significant.

QUESTION 12

What impact, if any, has the Securities and Exchange Commission (SEC) software moratorium had on your company?

The moratorium applies only to software intended for sale, so it was expected that its effect on software user companies would be minimal. The responses to this question confirmed that assumption. Virtually none of the responding companies indicated that the moratorium had any impact on their company. One company indicated that the moratorium helped them to establish accounting guidelines. Another said that it caused them to defer the internal capitalization issue. A third company said it caused them to review practices. Another said that it may influence the capital budgeting decision in 1984. A few companies were unaware of any moratorium.

QUESTION 13

On which categories of software cost is the investment tax credit or R&D tax credit taken?

The response to question 13 shows that about 4 companies in 10 take the investment tax credit on purchased systems (44.9 percent) and applications (41.7 percent) software, and a much smaller percentage take the credit for internally constructed systems (2.3 percent) and applications (3.2 percent) software. The IRS treats software as intangible and, therefore, not eligible for the investment tax credit unless the software is bundled with the hardware.[2] However, at least one court case has held that magnetic computer tapes are tangible property qualifying for the investment tax credit.[3]

About one company in three takes the R&D tax credit for internally constructed systems (35.6 percent) and applications (37.0 percent) software, and a much smaller percentage of respondents take the credit for purchased systems (10.6 percent) and applications (10.6 percent) software.

QUESTION 14

How is software classified for federal, sales/use, and property tax purposes?

The IRS classifies software as intangible unless it is bundled with hardware, so it may be inferred that a large portion of the 51.4 percent of respondents that classify software as tangible do so because it is bundled with hardware. However, some companies may classify separately priced software as tangible in order to take advantage of the investment tax credit. Furthermore, at least one court case has ruled that the full value of magnetic tapes is eligible for the investment tax credit.

For sales, use, and property tax purposes, software is classified as tangible or intangible based on statutory or case law. Tangible property is generally subject to tax, whereas intangible property generally is not. For sales/use tax, the respondents were about evenly divided between tangible (43.5 percent) and intangible (56.5 percent) treatment. Companies doing business in several states may have checked both responses, since the classification differs by state.

For personal property tax purposes, the vast majority (70.9 percent) classify software as intangible, which seems to be in conflict with the responses given to the sales/use tax question. Another complicating factor is that some states classify "canned" software as tangible and "custom" software as intangible.

A comparison of the vendor responses to the software-user responses reveals that vendors are far more likely to classify software as intangible for both federal and state purposes than are software users.

QUESTION 15

Is the same software item ever capitalized for financial statement purposes and expensed for tax purposes? Capitalized for tax purposes and expensed for financial statement purposes?

The vast majority of companies treat software expenditures the same for tax and financial statement purposes. For those companies which give different treatments, the primary reasons for capitalizing for financial statement purposes and expensing for tax purposes were:

1. Foreign tax regulations must be considered for multinational corporations.
2. Costs incurred for company personnel are expensed for tax and capitalized for book. Capitalization of these expenses is not accepted under IRS guidelines.
3. High cost of a single large applications project.
4. Impact on reported net income and EPS.
5. Cash flow and EPS.

6. The cost of certain major, multi-year projects are capitalized for financial statement purposes, because they are material to the sponsoring organization. Such costs are expensed for tax purposes, because they are not material on a companywide basis.
7. Aside from software bundled with hardware, only major systems—for example those costing in excess of $2 million—are capitalized for books. Policy is to generally expense all systems for tax and not request permission to capitalize. For tax, systems are only capitalized as a result of IRS audits or if bundled with hardware.
8. Only internally constructed software is treated differently for book and tax. The company is a cash basis taxpayer.
9. For tax purposes, Section 174 of the Internal Revenue Code permits deduction of these expenditures. For financial statement purposes, these expenditures have continuing benefit.
10. Internally constructed software is being capitalized on the financial statements, but is being expensed on the tax return to be consistent with Rev. Proc. 69-21.

The primary reasons for capitalizing for tax purposes and expensing for financial statement purposes were:

1. Financial accounting procedures treat purchased software costs as items of expense unless circumstances arise involving significant software purchase costs. Tax accounting procedures treat purchased software costs as capitalized items the cost of which is to be recovered by amortization deductions ratably over a period of five years, as per Rev. Proc. 69-21, 1969-2 C.B. 303.
2. Occasional large expenditures for purchased software are expensed for financial statement purposes to reflect conservative accounting and are capitalized for tax purposes to demonstrate the matching concept.
3. Capitalization is required for tax purposes.
4. Systems are capitalized as a result of IRS audits or if bundled with hardware.
5. IRS regulations require capitalization.
6. All software is capitalized for tax purposes. Software expenditures less than a specified threshold amount are expensed for financial statement purposes.

QUESTION 16

If software is capitalized for both financial statement and tax purposes, are the amortization method and time period used the same?

The vast majority (79.7 percent) of firms responding to this question use the same amortization method and time period for capitalized software for tax and financial reporting purposes. Where a different amortization method or time period are used, reasons given were:

1. The Accelerated Cost Recovery System is used for tax purposes.
2. Tax treatment is non-GAAP and is chosen to maximize tax benefits.
3. Company policy is to amortize purchased software over three years, while for tax purposes it is amortized over 60 months as required.
4. Company policy is to use the straight-line method for financial reporting and an accelerated method for tax purposes.
5. Tax law specifies straight-line amortization method.

QUESTION 17

What impact, if any, will the proposed Treasury Regulations on research and experimental expenditures, if adopted, have on your company with respect to software (reported in the Federal Register January 21, 1983, page 2799, right column)?

Many respondents did not feel that the proposed Treasury Regulations on research and experimental expenditures would have a significant effect on their company. The following comments were made:

1. While the planned projects would continue, some of the cost justification for various current and future projects would be weakened.
2. We might back off on our position that it is tangible personal property; we might not take the investment tax credit.
3. The proposed regulation will have an unfavorable impact, since costs of constructing computer software are not considered section 174 expenses, unless the program involves significant risks that it cannot be written.
4. Impact would be adverse, as it would restrict software available for the R&D credit.
5. It will keep us from claiming an R&D credit.
6. Our company could not claim R&D credits. This could affect policies on acquisition method and project profitability results.

QUESTION 18

If your primary business is manufacturing or transportation, annual sales for the most recent fiscal year were _____. If your primary business is Financial services or a public utility, assets at the end of the most recent fiscal year were _____.

Nearly half (48.0 percent) of the respondents were manufacturing or transportation companies with annual sales in excess of $1 billion, with the remainder divided among smaller manufacturing and transportation companies (23.7 percent) and financial service companies and public utilities (28.3 percent).

QUESTION 19

What type of business do you consider your company to be primarily involved in?

Most respondents were primarily involved in manufacturing (66.2 percent), followed by financial services (25.4 percent), other (7.0 percent), and other services (1.4 percent).

CHAPTER 6

The Effects of Software Accounting Policy on Bank Lending Decisions

Background

During the course of the interviews, several interviewees expressed the view that the inability to place software costs on the balance sheet would adversely affect a software firm's ability to raise capital. This feeling was reinforced by the responses received to a questionnaire that was sent to software-vendor companies. In the questionnaire, 48.5 percent of privately held software companies and 30.2 percent of the public companies surveyed agreed that the inability to include software costs on the balance sheet adversely affects the ability to raise capital.

The view that accounting policy affects a company's stock price or the ability to raise debt capital has been expressed a number of times in the literature. In 1965, J. L. O'Donnell examined the price earnings ratio trend of 37 public utilities for the period 1949–61 and determined that accounting policy can affect stock price.[1] His second study produced the same result.[2] On the other hand, Edward L. Summers studied the effect of investment tax credit, interperiod tax allocation, and funds flow statements of stock prices in the airline industry and found no statistically significant impact.[3] George J. Staubus, in studying the association between several accounting variables and stock price, found that investors found income before depreciation to be more useful than income after depreciation.[4]

An experimental study conducted by R. E. Jensen concluded that variations in depreciation and inventory accounting policies affected analysts' opinions.[5] W. J. Bruns, Jr., concluded that inventory policy does not affect pricing, advertising, and production decisions.[6] The three studies that T. R. Dyckman conducted reached conflicting results. His first study concluded that variations in inventory methods can influence financial statement readers—a conclusion that is diametrically opposed to that reached by Bruns.[7] Dyckman's second study[8] concluded that inventory method does not influence decision making, but his third study[9] reached the opposite conclusion. Dopuch and Ronen, using students as financial-statement readers, concluded that inventory policy does influence readers of financial statements.[10] Mlynarczyk's study comparing the flow-through and deferred method of tax accounting reached the same conclusion.[11] Falk and Ophir found that investors react both to the content and form of disclosure.[12]

There have been at least three major studies dealing with the effect of accounting policies on bank lending decisions.[13] In 1970, T. N. Jain conducted a study of the effects of tax-accounting methods on bank lending decisions.[14] In that study, financial data for two companies were sent to 110 lending officers at large banks. The high response rate of 67 percent (74 responses) was due, in part, to the fact that most of the bankers were also contacted personally, and a follow-up letter was sent to the remainder. The financial data for the two companies was identical in all respects except for the method of accounting for income taxes; one company used comprehensive allocation, and one used partial allocation. The study found that the method of accounting for income taxes does influence lending decisions.

The second study was conducted by A. A. El-Arabi in 1977.[15] In this study, two sets of financial statements were prepared for two hypothetical firms. The data for both sets of financial statements were identical except for the accounting principles used. One set used the FIFO method of inventory valuation and the straight-line depreciation method. The second used LIFO and the sum-of-the-years-digits method. The sample consisted of two groups of banks. Group one consisted of 332 banks (of which 37 percent responded) and was sent the FIFO/straight-line data. Group two consisted of 331 banks (of which 32 percent responded) and was sent the LIFO/SYD data. The study found that the accounting principles used did affect the lending decision.

The third study was conducted by M. M. El-Maksy.[16] In this study, 1,050 loan officers from 240 banks were divided into seven groups. Responses were received from 267 lenders representing 143 banks. The first group received financial data containing no *FASB No. 33* information. Each of the treatment groups received one piece of *FASB No. 33* data (either constant dollar, current cost, or both) which was either presented in the notes to the financial statements or on the face of the income statement and notes. The study found that lending decisions for the control group were not significantly different statistically than those for the treatment groups, although lending decisions for the treatment groups were less favorable than those for the control groups in 94 percent of the cases. The groups receiving constant dollar data made lending decisions that were not significantly different statistically from those decisions made by lenders who received current cost data.

The Present Study

Upon completion of the interviews with executives of software vendor firms, it was decided that a questionnaire should be mailed to bank lending officers to determine whether the software accounting policy a company has affects its ability to raise debt capital. Two questionnaires and related financial data were mailed to two separate groups of commercial lending officers, chosen from banks having at least $500 million in assets. Data for Campbell Corporation, a company that capitalizes software costs with net income of $2,552,107, $2,213,154, and $903,131 for 1982, 1981, and 1980, respectively, was sent to 174 commercial lending officers. Campbell Corporation is a real, publicly held software company. The financial data sent was authentic. Only the company name was changed.

Data for Edwards Corporation was sent to 174 other commercial lending officers. The only difference between Edwards and Campbell was that Edwards expenses all software costs. Edwards had a $2,103,000 net loss in 1982 and net income of $498,000 and $301,000 in 1981 and 1980, respectively.

Twenty responses were received for Campbell and 30 for Edwards. Responses to the individual questions are summarized below.

QUESTION 1

How large a line of credit would your bank be willing to grant to this company?

Table 1 summarizes the responses. Twenty-five percent of the commercial lending officers responding to the Campbell questionnaire would not grant a line of credit, compared with 57 percent of those responding to Edwards. For those who would grant a line of credit, the amounts ranged as high as $7.5 million for Campbell and $15 million for Edwards. A test of variability determined that the responses received from the two groups was not statistically different at the 10 percent level, even though the reject rate for Edwards (57 percent) was more than twice that for Campbell (25 percent). Perhaps this result is due to the low response rate and high degree of variability.

TABLE 1

Campbell Corporation		Edwards Corporation	
Number of Responses	Amount of Credit ($ millions)	Number of Responses	Amount of Credit ($ millions)
5	-0-	17	-0-
1	$.75-1	1	1
1	1	1	3-6
1	1-2	1	4
2	2	1	4.5
3	3	6	5
1	3.5	1	6
1	4.5	1	10
2	5	1	10-15
2	7		
1	7.5		
20		30	

QUESTION 2

If your bank would not approve a line of credit for this company, please indicate why the application would be denied.

The banks denying Campbell's application responded as follows:

1. Too many questions raised in financial statements—for example, purpose of line (to replace other bank?), carry receivables, carry proprietary software costs? We also question the quality of the financial statements: there is no cash/funds flow, no reconcilement of net worth, no amortization of property and equipment on the income statement, capitalized leases do not appear to be on the balance sheet, and write-off of computer costs (in 4-6 years) does not appear to be taking place on P&L.

2. All needs appear to be permanent financing. It is impossible to determine if a line can be repaid by the liquidation of short term assets.

3. Concerns: leverage, vulnerability of main product line in competitive environment; bulk of assets (computers and software) could become obsolete rapidly.

4. The application would be denied until further information concerning the following could be obtained: an accounts receivable aging; projections indicating future profitability, capital expenditures, and the direction of the company. This would include projected income statements and balance sheets. We would also need a recent interim statement and a sources and uses of funds statement dated December 31, 1982.

5. Interest expense on bonds will be 11 percent of $20 million, or $2.2 million, which would entirely deplete earnings based on 1982 figures.

The banks denying Edward's application responded as follows:

1. Prior to my bank venturing a decision regarding this company's ability to receive from us a line of credit and/or a term loan, more in-depth analysis would need to be made. Certainly, we would wish to view pro forma balance sheets (five years) and income statements (five years). The pro formas would aid us in obtaining some insight into the company's future financial needs and management objectives.

The tremendous sales growth that the company has enjoyed during the past five years has certainly been a contributing force in the company's need for external funds. The pro formas that the bank would require would aid us in determining how much of the external funds would be needed to support the increased receivables and inventory (short term), and how much external funds would be needed to support the increase in fixed assets (long term).

If the company's projections reveal a continuation of the rapid sales growth, we could conclude that repayment of a portion of the external funds would not be repaid until the rate of sales growth declines. Of course, those funds that will support the receivables and inventory will be considered to be self-liquidating.

We would request a break out of the general and administrative (G&A) expenses so as to better calculate the company's G&A trends. Depreciation expense is needed to better analyze the company's cash flow and to calculate more revealing ratios.

The company's sales growth and interest expenses were very important in the decline of profitability for the Edwards Corporation. Next year, the servicing of the debenture, interest, and sinking fund will add additional strain to profitability.

2. There is a significant increase in long-term subordinated convertible debt with sinking fund requirements of $1.5 million. Long-term debt should provide a sufficient operating fund for the near term. There is no explanation for the loss other than increased cost of goods sold.

3. The company is not generating sufficient cash to support its current financing costs.

4. (a) Nature of business, **(b)** operating deficiencies; **(c)** risk of upcoming year; **(d)** uncertain nature of accounts receivable, operating expenses, and payable and subordination convertible debentures; **(e)** increasing international business.

5. In general, we do not make loans without firsthand knowledge and assessment of management. In particular it is not clear what the purpose of the line would be given their present abundance of cash resources.

6. (a) Severe operating loss due to excessive increase in expenses; **(b)** insufficient financial data regarding expenses; **(c)** heavy current and long-term credit obligations; **(d)** no knowledge of management and its ability; **(e)** no interim financial data for any portion of 1983.

7. (a) Revenue recognition methods; **(b)** product is subject to obsolescence without warning.

8. (a) The investment in the building is too much for the company to carry (interest plus depreciation); **(b)** the three-year life on computers used until 1981 was too long, and the company has not shown an operating profit since the change.

9. (a) Insufficient information; **(b)** source and application of funds statement for 1982 was not given; **(c)** value or potential future income in program library being developed, market penetration and permanence for one to five years; **(d)** this company is highly leveraged, and if present liquidity is used, there will be no place to go except lender-financial losses with no valuable assets to liquidate.

10. The company is unable to generate operating profit. Cash flow is inadequate. Speculation is that the company is having to discount below costs to meet competition.

11. (a) Downward trend in savings; **(b)** no clear source of repayment; **(c)** no evident secondary source of repayment; **(d)** a $6 million revolver is already in place.

12. There is a question as to the quality of receivables. An aging schedule would be helpful. The line of business makes the company a high-risk venture.

13. The company is insolvent based on the times-interest-earned ratio. It is also highly leveraged. Declining profitability and insufficient cash flow add to this credit risk. The company also has future debt obligations that would further deter its ability to service its debt.

14. (a) Volatile industry; **(b)** weak operating earnings; **(c)** excessive fixed-asset expansion for a company that does not have excess cash to allocate to fixed assets, and the nature of which does not require ownership of land and buildings—the company can operate from leased facilities; **(d)** the company incurred operating losses that will be compounded by the interest expense on the additional debt; **(e)** evidence of unsound judgment on the part of management.

15. (a) Existing $6 million line of credit; **(b)** deteriorating profits; **(c)** receivables collection.

16. Account-receivable turnover is slow (over 100 days). With an operating loss experienced in 1982, the company could be running into a situation of evergreen credit.

QUESTION 3

What rate of interest would you charge (for an unsecured line of credit)?

Table 2 summarizes the response to this question. Interest rates have been adjusted to take compensating balances into account. A test of variability revealed that there was not a significant difference (at the 10 percent level) between the rate charged Campbell and that charged to Edwards. This finding concurs with that found in the Jain study.[17]

TABLE 2

Campbell Corporation		Edwards Corporation	
Number of Responses	Interest Rate*	Number of Responses	Interest Rate*
5	N.A.	16	N.A.
1	11.00	1	11.00
1	11.25	4	12.00
1	11.58	1	12.63
2	12.00	1	12.75
1	12.22	1	12.78
1	12.50	1	13.16
1	12.78	4	13.33
1	13.00	1	15.00
1	13.06		
1	13.16		
2	13.33		
1	13.53		
1	13.75		
20		30	

*The interest rate given was adjusted to take into account any compensating balance that would be required. The prime rate was 11 percent at the time the questionnaire was mailed, and the rate did not change until after all responses had been received.

QUESTION 4

What additional terms would you impose?

The response to this question varied widely but included the following items:

1. Compensating balance ranging from 5–15 percent, and/or a commitment fee ranging from ⅛ percent to ½ percent.

2. Credit line granted up to 60–75 percent of accounts receivable; receive account receivable aging schedule monthly.

3. Loan secured by inventory or other assets; security agreement on property, equipment, and/or receivables.

4. Quarterly financial data; 90-day review.

5. Convert line to term loan with 3–5 year payout.

6. Annual cleanup with zero balance for 30–60 days.

7. Restrictions on capital expenditures, lease obligations, working capital, dividends, additional debt, bonuses, officers' salaries, changes in ownership.

8. Require owner guarantee, approval of subordinated debt holders, key insurance.

QUESTION 5

If, instead of a line of credit, the company had applied for a $2,000,000, five-year loan, would your bank grant the loan?

Table 3 summarizes the responses to this question. Although a larger percentage of lending officers said they would lend to Campbell than to Edwards, the chi-square test indicated that this difference was not significant at the 10-percent level.

TABLE 3

	Campbell Corporation		Edwards Corporation	
	Number of Responses	Percentage	Number of Responses	Percentage
Yes	10	50%	9	30%
No	10	50	21	70
	20		30	

QUESTION 6

Do you consider this loan to be extremely risky, risky, marginal, safe, or extremely safe?

Table 4 shows that bankers tended to view a loan to Edwards as more risky than one to Campbell. The chi-square test indicated that this difference was significant at the 10-percent level.

TABLE 4

Loan Considered to Be	Campbell Corporation		Edwards Corporation	
	Number of Responses	Percentage	Number of Responses	Percentage
Extremely risky	2	10%	7	23%
Risky	4	20	12	40
Marginal	5	25	9	30
Safe	9	45	2	7
Extremely safe	0	0	0	0
Totals	20		30	

QUESTION 7

If your bank would not approve this term loan, please indicate why the application would be denied.

The responses to this question were similar to those given for Question 2.

QUESTION 8

What rate of interest would you charge for the term loan?

TABLE 5

Campbell Corporation		Edwards Corporation	
Number of Responses	Interest Rate*	Number of Responses	Interest Rate*
10	N.A.	21	N.A.
1	11.75	2	12.00
2	12.11	1	12.50
3	13.33	2	13.33
1	13.50	1	13.68
1	13.61	1	13.89
1	13.89	2	15.29
1	14.69		
20		30	

*The interest rate given was adjusted to take into account any compensating balance that would be required. The prime rate was 11 percent at the time the questionnaire was mailed, and the rate did not change until after all responses had been received.

Table 5 summarizes the responses to this question. The average interest rate charged to Campbell is 13.165 percent, compared to 13.473 percent for Edwards. Although the rate charged Edwards is somewhat higher than that charged Campbell, the difference is not significant at the 10-percent level.[18]

QUESTION 9

What compensating balance would be required?

Of the 10 banks that would grant a term loan to Campbell, 8 would require a compensating balance, ranging from 5 to 20 percent and averaging 9.7 percent. Of the nine banks that would lend to Edwards, six would require a compensating balance, ranging from 5 to 15 percent and averaging 10.6 percent.

QUESTION 10

What restrictions on working capital would be imposed?

Of the 10 bankers that would lend to Campbell, 3 would require a minimum of $10 million in working capital and 1 would require $5 million. One bank would require that the current level ($10,614,400) be maintained. Others would require a current ratio of 1.5:1 to 2.1:1 or a working capital/asset ratio of 18 percent or a working capital/revenue ratio of 35 percent. One bank would place no restrictions on working capital. Responses for the Edwards corporation were similar. Tables 6 and 7 provide a more detailed breakdown of the responses for both companies.

QUESTION 11

How much additional debt would the company be permitted to incur?

Five of the 10 Campbell responses would not allow additional long-term debt without bank approval. Two banks would allow an additional $1 million; one bank would allow an additional $5 million. Two banks would require a debt/worth ratio of 2.0:1. (See also Tables 6 and 7.)

Of the nine Edwards responses, six would not permit additional debt. One bank would not place a restriction on additional debt. Another would allow $2.5 million for each of the next five years. One would require a 3.0:1 debt-to-worth ratio.

QUESTION 12

What is the maximum annual dividend that could be paid?

Four of the 10 Campbell responses would not permit any dividends. One bank would impose no restrictions on dividends. Other respondents would allow dividends ranging from 10-50 percent of net income or cash flow.

TABLE 6
Banks Approving a Term Loan for Campbell Corporation—Summary of Restrictions

Bank No.	Question 10 Working Capital	Question 11 Additional Debt	Question 12 Maximum Annual Dividend	Question 13 Additional Terms
1.	$5 million minimum.	$5 million.	None.	Term loan agreement with usual covenants.
2.	$10 million minimum.	No long-term debt of more than $1 million without bank approval.	No response.	Liability to stockholders equity ratio not more than 1.8:1; no capital expenditures in excess of $1 million or purchase of treasury stock without bank approval.
3.	$10 million minimum.	None without permission, including additional leases.	None without permission.	Negative pledge on assets, no change in management, limit capital expenditures and lease commitments.
4.	Not to go below current levels ($10.6 million).	None without bank approval.	None without bank approval.	Net worth and liquidity tests.
5.	Working capital as a percentage of assets should be maintained at 18 percent.	Debt-to-worth ratio should not exceed 2.0 in 1983, 1.8 in 1984, and 1.7 in 1985 and	10 percent of net profit after taxes.	Secured by fixed assets.

6.	Current ratio 1.5:1, working capital 35 percent of revenues.	should continue to improve over the 5-year period.	10 percent of net cash flow from operations after long-term debt service.	No net increase to fixed assets; courseware construction costs net balance maintained at 45 percent (or less) of annual dollar sales rate; quarterly financials.
7.	$10 million minimum.	Debt-to-worth ratio not to exceed 2.0:1, no additional long-term debt without approval.	None.	No dividends or outside debt financing without prior approval. Not to be used for working capital.
8.	Maintain current ratio (2.2:1).	Up to $1 million more, depending on use and need.	30 percent net after tax.	None stated.
9.	No restrictions.	None.	No restrictions.	Should be secured, guaranty of 20 percent stockholders, loan agreement, key insurance if necessary.
10.	Minimum current ratio 2.0:1.	Depends on purpose and ratio trends.	50 percent of net income.	None stated.

TABLE 7
Banks Approving a Term Loan for Edwards Corporation—Summary of Restrictions

Bank No.	Question 10 Working Capital	Question 11 Additional Debt	Question 12 Maximum Annual Dividend	Question 13 Additional Terms
1.	Required quick ratio 1.75:1, current ratio 2.00:1.	None.	None.	Security agreements on property and equipment, accounts receivable; $2 million guarantee of payment.
2.	Minimum current ratio of 2:1 and working capital minimum $10 million.	None without approval.	None.	Profitability within a predetermined time frame, actual performance tracking closely to projected, maximum leverage, negative pledge on assets, no other debt, dividends, no treasury stock purchases, no asset dispositions or mergers or acquisition unless prior approval given.
3.	1.2 current ratio, $8 million minimum.	None.	One year after profitable operations, 25 percent of after-tax earnings.	Limit capital expenditures; leverage covenants-step up over course of loan; earnings recapture.
4.	$7 million minimum.	No other senior debt or capital leases without prior bank approval.	None, without prior bank approval.	Net worth floor of $11 million; no capital expenditures above a certain amount without approval; security, possibly, if no good evidence of turnaround.

5.	Maintain 1.75:1 current ratio.	None without bank approval.	Dependent on earnings and cash flow.	No borrowings from other sources, no pledging of any assets, minimum working capital ratio, maximum debt-to-worth ratio, quarterly financial statements.
6.	$7 million minimum.	No restriction stated.	No restriction stated.	At the end of 2 years, if the company has not returned to profitable operations, the bank would reserve the right to restructure debt repayment.
7.	1.75:1 current ratio, $5 million minimum.	$2.5 million each year for next 5 years.	25 percent of earnings.	Maximum debt-to-worth ratio of 2.00:1.
8.	Secured by fixed assets with an 80 percent advance.	Must maintain debt-to-worth ratio of 3.00:1.	Allowed if debt-to-worth ratio remains 2.5:1 or below.	None stated.
9.	1.75:1 current ratio, 7.5 million minimum.	No additional debt without bank approval other than normal trade payables.	None.	Security agreements on accounts receivables, all machinery, equipment, furniture, fixtures, second lien on all previously encumbered fixed assets; restrictive covenants on capital accounts.

Four of the nine Edwards responses would not permit dividends. Two others would permit dividends up to 25 percent of earnings. One would require a debt-to-worth ratio of 2.5:1. (See also Tables 6 and 7.)

QUESTION 13

What additional terms would you impose?

Most bankers would impose additional terms for both Campbell and Edwards. The additional terms are summarized in Tables 6 and 7.

QUESTION 14

The bank's total assets are _____.

Total Assets	Campbell	Edwards
More than $5 billion	5	4
$5 billion or less	15	26
Total	20	30

A correlation between bank size and other questionnaire responses was not made due to the small sample size.[19]

QUESTION 15

The person completing this questionnaire has had _____ years experience in a loan department.

Years	Campbell	Edwards
2 or less	9	9
More than 2, less than 5	0	3
5–10	8	11
More than 10	2	6
No response	1	1
Total	20	30

A correlation between years of loan experience and other questionnaire responses was not made due to the small sample size.[20]

QUESTION 16

The person completing this questionnaire is a(n) _____ (title or position).

Position	Campbell	Edwards
Senior or executive vice president or other senior officer	0	4
Vice president, secretary or treasurer	5	11
Assistant vice president or other assistant officer	12	13
Not an officer	3	2
Total	20	30

A correlation between title and other questionnaire responses was not made due to the small sample size.[21]

QUESTION 17

The office where this questionnaire is being completed is located in the _____ (area).

Office Location	Campbell	Edwards
Northeast	1	8
South	10	9
North Central	6	8
West	2	4
No response	1	1
Total	20	30

A correlation between geographic location and other questionnaire responses was not made due to the small sample size.[22]

Summary and Conclusions

Companies that do not capitalize software costs find it more difficult to raise debt capital than companies that do capitalize such costs. This fact was brought to the author's attention during the course of the interviews with executives from software vending companies and was reinforced by the responses received on the software vendor questionnaire, which revealed that a substantial proportion of software vendor company executives feel that not capitalizing software costs hinders their ability to raise debt capital. Furthermore, the response to Question 6 of the banker questionnaire (Campbell/Edwards) indicated that bank lending officers view a loan to a company that expenses software costs as more risky than a loan to a company that capitalizes software costs.

Although not significant at the 10-percent level, some of the responses to the other questions in the banker questionnaire lead in the same direction. Seventeen of 30 (57 percent) lending officers would not grant a line of credit to Edwards, compared to 5 out of 20 (25 percent) for Campbell. Question 2 revealed that one of the main reasons for the hesitancy to lend was the weak operating performance of Edwards, which several banks mentioned as a reason for not lending to Edwards, while none of the bankers that received the Campbell questionnaire gave poor operating performance as a reason for not granting a line of credit to Campbell. Due to the company's software accounting policy, Campbell showed 1982 net income of $2,552,107, compared with a 1982 loss of $2,103,000 for Edwards.

For those banks that would lend to Campbell or Edwards, the rate of interest charged, although not significant at the 10-percent level, is higher for Edwards than for Campbell.

	Campbell	Edwards
Q 3. Interest rate charged for a line of credit	12.566%	12.760%
Q 8. Interest rate charged for a term loan	13.165	13.473

When asked whether the bank would grant a $2 million term loan, half of the Campbell bankers responded that they would, compared to 30 percent for Edwards.

The interviews and questionnaire responses point to one conclusion: a company that capitalizes software costs will find it easier to raise debt capital than will a company that expenses these costs.[23]

CHAPTER 7

Taxation of Software

Background

Prior to mid-1969, state taxation of computer software was not an issue. Companies that sold hardware included the software at no extra charge. The price of the software was "bundled" with that of the hardware. In 1969, International Business Machines Corporation (IBM) became the first major hardware manufacturer to state separately the price of its hardware and software.[1] The decision to separately state the price of hardware and software was partially in response to antitrust pressure.[2] As a result of IBM's announcement, a new industry developed—that of software manufacturing. As of the end of 1983, there are more than 4,000 independent manufacturers of software in the United States alone. Many of these firms are small in terms of revenue and are privately held, but some software manufacturers are publicly owned and are among the *Fortune 1000*.

Since the unbundling of software in the late 1960s a series of controversies have developed, primarily revolving around the issue of whether software is tangible or intangible for state sales, use, and property tax purposes, as well as for federal tax purposes.[3] If software is classified as tangible personal property, it is generally subject to state sales, use, and property taxation. If intangible, it is generally exempt. As of late 1983, 33 states assess a sales or use tax on prewritten programs, and 20 states do so for custom programs.[4] One reason for the difference in tax treatment is that standardized programs are sometimes viewed as a product or "good," whereas custom programming is looked upon as a service in some states.

The advent of the taxation of the sale of software has generated much controversy.[5] Part of the problem lies in the fact that there seems to be more than one acceptable definition of "software," and there is no clear-cut line that distinguishes a software product or good within the meaning of the Uniform Commercial Code (UCC) from a service, or even, in some cases, what distinguishes "software" from "hardware."[6] We now turn to that issue.

What Is Software?

In order to analyze the various methods of accounting for software, it might be good to start with a definition of software. Unfortunately, no single definition is currently undisputably accepted. Software might be defined as the programs that tell the computer what to do. Or, it might be defined as total data processing expenditures less hardware, communications, and supply costs. Another definition might be total data processing personnel costs plus the costs associated with the purchase or lease of computer programs developed by outside organizations. Software cost might also include the portion of hardware expenditures that reflect the bundled operating-system component. Certain end-user expenditures might also be included in the definition of software costs.

The most broad definition would be that software includes everything that is not hardware, which would include manuals and other educational materials as well as personnel training program costs and hardware maintenance costs.[7]

Computer hardware is generally thought to consist of the physical equipment that actually makes up the computer system, such as the central processing unit, input and output devices, and an information storage center.[8]

The Computer Dictionary and Handbook has defined software as:

> 1. The internal programs or routines professionally prepared to simplify programming and computer operations. . . .
> 2. Various programming aids that are frequently supplied by the manufacturers to facilitate the purchaser's efficient operation of the equipment. Such software items include various assemblers, generators, subroutine libraries, compilers, operating systems, and industry-application programs.[9]

Frank has defined software as:

> [T]hat which could be invoked by hardware . . . software includes the design and development of computer programs as well as their maintenance. It does not include the costs associated with operations.[10]

The Internal Revenue Service (IRS) defines computer software as:

> [A]ll programs or routines used to cause a computer to perform a desired task or set of tasks, and the documentation required to describe and maintain those programs. Computer programs of all classes, for example, operating systems, executive systems, monitors, compilers and translators, assembly routines, and

utility programs as well as application programs are included. "Computer software" does not include procedures which are external to computer operations, such as instructions to transcription operators and external control procedures.[11]

The definition of software promulgated by the National Bureau of Standards[12] and adopted by the U.S. Bureau of Standards[13] is: "Computer programs, procedures, rules, and possibly associated documentation concerned with the operation of a data processing system."

Several courts and state legislatures have also defined software. Some have even made distinctions between systems software and applications software. The Supreme Court of Tennessee has defined a systems (operational) program as one that is fundamental to the functioning of the hardware, or software that controls the hardware and makes it run.[14]

Bryant and Mather state that systems software consists of:

> 1. Compilers, which are used to translate symbolic code into machine language, and which are also capable of replacing a series of instructions with subroutines.
> 2. Sorts, which assemble and file items of data in a certain sequence or order.
> 3. Utility routines, which perform functions such as transferring data from one magnetic tape to another.[15]

Applications software was viewed as performing useful tasks, such as employee payrolls or loan amortization schedules.[16] Accounts receivable, payable, inventory, and even home computer command modules, diskette, and cassette programs would be included under this category.

The reason for this systems/applications distinction is due to tax treatment. Systems software may be regarded as an integral part of the hardware, therefore, making it tangible property subject to tax in some jurisdictions.[17] Applications software is treated by some jurisdictions as intangible property not subject to taxation.

Anthony G. Ferraro has defined hardware and software as follows:

> Hardware consists of the electronic components and mechanical components that comprise a series of machines which have the ability to interpret and follow software instructions to produce a useful product. Software consists of programs that are used to operate the machine to make the system produce a desirable result. Hardware cannot perform functions for which it was designed without a software program.
>
> There are two kinds of software, both consisting of tangible instructions. They differ only in their intended purpose. One is called "operational" software, and the other is called "utility" or "application" software. Operational systems software is the written operating instructions, programmed into tape, for the purpose of making a computer operational. For example, a computer has operational software programs so that it will function as determined by the design and the engineering of the particular computer. These same software

instructions would be furnished to all users of that same type of equipment. The expense of this basic engineering cost is the same as the engineering cost of any other operational program. Whether the cost is handled as an engineering expense or as a software cost is merely a matter of company policy.

Application or utility software is designed to allow the specific user better to utilize the equipment. The cost of materials and labor to develop the systems analyses, systems designs and programs are all part of the computer software program. This involves endless man-hours whereby these products are outlined, established, debugged, and tested.[18]

In the same journal, Karl Heinzman describes software as follows:

"Software" may be very broadly defined as a collection of instructions of programs (such as assemblers, compilers, utility routines, application programs and operating systems) which are fed into a computer to tell it what to do. There are two types of computer programs or procedures (software) which must be recognized:
1. Those which have to do with the operation of a computer, sometimes called basic software, system control programs or computer operational software (operational software).
2. Those which have to do with the implementation of a system, procedures or computer applications which are sometimes referred to as application programs, product programs, custom software services or computer application software (application software).[19]

Some state legislatures have split hairs even further by distinguishing an "off-the-shelf" or "canned" program from a "custom" program.[20] A canned program is one that is sold to several users, whereas a customized program is written for one user according to that user's specifications. However, problems of definition can develop when a seller of software makes changes in a canned program to meet the requirements of one particular user. How extensive can the changes be before the canned program becomes a customized program?

The Financial Accounting Standards Board (FASB) has issued an interpretation[21] and a technical bulletin[22] on the topic of software accounting. Neither publication defines software, although they do state that, for accounting purposes, software costs need not always be treated as research and development costs which must be expensed. Unfortunately, neither pronouncement clearly states when "software costs" (whatever that term means) can be capitalized and amortized for financial accounting purposes.

With all these conflicting and inconsistent definitions of software being offered by various private groups, federal agencies, state legislatures, and a multitude of courts, it is no wonder that the issue of software has become so complex. And, it appears as though the conflicts involving software will not be resolved at any time in the near future. As technology continues to evolve the very nature of software will also change. Already a hybrid form called "firmware" has evolved, which is separate and distinct from both hardware and software.[23]

Tangible versus Intangible

The primary issue in software tax cases is tangibility. If software is viewed as tangible it is often subject to state sales, use, and property taxes; if classified as intangible, it is often exempt from tax. Several lines of legal reasoning have been used to justify classifying software as intangible and, therefore, exempt from tax.

The "knowledge" rationale and the "personal service" rationale were both used in *District of Columbia* v. *Universal Computer Associates*, the first case to address the taxability (and tangibility) of computer software.[24] In that case, a custom program and a canned program were held to be intangible property and, therefore, not subject to the personal property tax. The reasoning was that it was the intangible information contained on the cards that was being purchased and not the cards themselves. Once the information contained on the cards was transferred into the computer, all that remained was the knowledge, which is intangible.

Other cases have relied on a similar line of reasoning to justify the classification of software as intangible. In a Tennessee case, it was held that both systems and applications software are intangible in cases where the tangible medium used (card, tape, disk, and so forth) is either returned to the seller or destroyed.[25] The reasoning is that the property purchased is actually intangible knowledge, and the use of a tangible medium to transfer that intangible knowledge is "merely incidental to the purchase of the intangible knowledge and information stored on the tapes."[26]

Other courts have expanded on the knowledge rationale first espoused in *Universal Computer Associates* and *Commerce Union Bank* v. *Tidwell*. The "essence of the transaction" test was applied by the Texas Supreme Court three years after *Tidwell*.[27] Following the reasoning of the District of Columbia Circuit Court and the Tennessee Supreme Court, the Texas court held that, where the transaction is in essence the purchase of an intangible, such as a custom or canned program, the sale is exempt from the Texas sales tax, which only applies to the sale of tangible property.

The knowledge rationale, as applied in the District of Columbia, Tennessee, and Texas, classifies both custom and canned software as intangible; both systems and applications software are so classified.

The "relative value" test has also been applied to software tax cases.[28] This test recognizes software creation to be a process involving both tangible and intangible elements. Most of the value of a software product is attributable to the intellectual content; the tangible medium used to store and transfer this knowledge—cards, tapes, or disks—are incidental costs. Programs selling for $50,000 might be stored on tapes or disks costing under $50, so the purchaser of a program is actually buying knowledge rather than a physical product.

The "mode of transmission" test has also been applied in a number of cases.[29] This test has a few variations, but basically stands for the proposition that, where the knowledge can be conveyed from the seller to the buyer without the use of a physical medium, such as cards, tapes, or disks, the transaction involves the sale of intangible property. This transfer can occur, in theory at least, by having the seller's programmer give verbal instructions to the buyer's computer operator. A more practical approach, and one that is often used, is to transfer the program from the seller's computer to the buyer's computer directly, over telephone lines.[30] Using this mode of transmission can save $30,000 if the sale of a $500,000 program involves a 6 percent sales tax state, provided the sale would otherwise be taxable.[31]

Several courts have made the analogy of software programs to films and phonograph records.[32] Films and records have much in common with computer software, but several distinctions can be made as well. Most of the value of a film or record (or a book for that matter) is attributable to the intellectual and artistic content rather than the celluloid, plastic, or paper upon which that content is recorded.[33] Buyers of records and film (movie theaters) do not consider themselves to be purchasers of celluloid or plastic. However, one critical distinction is that the celluloid upon which the movie is recorded is "a crucial artistic element of the motion picture; without film there could be no movie."[34]

Another distinction that can be made between film and software is that the media upon which the computer program is recorded (cards, tapes, disks, and so forth) can be returned to the seller or destroyed after the program has been run through the computer; it is of no further use or value. Movie film, on the other hand, has continuing value after the movie has been shown; it can be used again and again.[35] In *Tidwell*, the court also made an analogy between a phonograph record, which is retained by the purchaser after use, and a computer tape, which is returned to the seller and is of no further use to the purchaser once the program has been run on the computer.[36]

Another distinction that has been made between software and films, records, and books is that the latter three items can be used immediately upon purchase, whereas software must first be translated into a language that can be understood by the computer.[37] Furthermore, the latter three items are immediately perceptible to the senses, whereas software, in essence, is not.[38]

Another distinction that has been made between software and films, records, and books is that the software sales or licensing agreement often includes periodic updating by the seller. Films, records, and books, on the other hand, are not updated after sale.[39] However, this distinction does not apply to the many programs that are not updated after sale.

Courts have also wrestled with the issue of whether the sale of computer software constitutes the sale of a product or a personal service. This issue is frequently raised in service bureau cases,[40] although analogies to the UCC[41] and the sale of information[42] have also been made. Generally speaking, if software is viewed as being a product or good, it is tangible property subject to sales, use, and property taxation. If viewed as a service, software is intangible and not subject to these taxes. Canned programs are more likely to be viewed as products than are custom programs, which involve more personal service. Software often involves elements of both sales and services, and courts have developed several tests to aid in making this distinction. One test is whether the transfer of property is necessary or merely convenient in order to achieve the primary purpose of the transaction.[43] Another test is whether the value of the materials is small compared to the value of the services.[44] A third test is whether the item transferred has value only to the purchaser, as is the case when a custom program is acquired, or whether the item can be sold to the general public, as is the case with canned programs.[45]

In the case of canned programs, no services are performed at all; they are sold off-the-shelf as is and are available to the general public. They are conveyed to the purchaser using a tangible medium, and there is no question that the transfer of the tangible property (cards, tapes, disks, and so on) is more than merely incidental to the transaction. In contrast, custom programs are different for a particular customer and are of no value to the general public. The value of the tangible medium is small in comparison with the value of the services required to write the custom program.

Before discussing the major cases that have been decided in the relatively new area of software taxation, a review of the oft-cited cases involving film, the sale of information, the Uniform Commercial Code, and computer service bureaus should be made, since the same reasoning regarding the tangibility and sale-versus-service issues applies to these areas.

The Film Cases

Film making and software creation have much in common. In both cases, the value of the product is derived almost entirely from the intellectual effort put forth. The celluloid upon which the film is recorded and the cards, tapes, or disks upon which software is recorded are incidental expenses. The purchaser of a film or software product is making the purchase for the intellectual content, not for the tangible property upon which the film or software is stored. Taxpayers have argued that this intangible purchase is not subject to the sales, use, or property tax.

In *United Artists Corp.* v. *Taylor*, the New York court, in holding that the New York City sales tax law applied to the lease of a movie film print, said:

> The transaction which is the subject of the tax under review consists of the transfer by the distributor to the exhibitor of the possession of corporeal property in the form of positive and negative prints of photoplays with the license to use or exhibit them for a specified time. The license to exhibit without the transfer of possession would be valueless. Together they are one transaction and constitute a sale within the definition of Local Law No. 24.[46]

In *Saenger Realty Corp* v. *Grosjean*, the Louisiana Supreme Court held that the operator of a movie theater was liable for the Louisiana sales tax and that the measure of the tax was the amount paid to the producer for the lease of the film print.[47]

The frequently cited case of *Crescent Amusement Co.* v. *Carson*, citing *United Artists* and *Saenger Realty*, held that the rental or leasing of motion picture films is a rental or leasing of tangible personal property within the meaning of the Tennessee Sales Tax Law and that the correct measure of the tax is the gross amount of rent paid, not the cost of the physical material in the film print.[48] The court stated that:

> There is scarcely to be found any article susceptible to sale or rent that is not the result of an idea, genius, skill and labor applied to a physical substance. A loaf of bread is the result of the skill and labor of the cook who mixed the physical ingredients and applied heat at the temperature and consistency her judgment dictated. A radio is the result of the thought of a genius, or of several such persons, combined with the skill and labor of trained technicians applied to a tangible mass of substance. An automobile is the result of all these elements, and of patents, etc.; and so on, ad infinitum. If these elements should be separated from the finished product and the sales tax applied only to the cost of the raw material, the sales tax act would, for all practical purposes, be entirely destroyed.[49]

In *Michael Todd Co.* v. *County of Los Angeles*, an ad valorem personal property tax was assessed against the Michael Todd Company on the film negatives of a copyrighted motion picture entitled "Around the World in Eighty Days."[50] A tax of $105,064.46 was levied, based on an estimated cash value of $1,526,900. Without copyright protection, the negatives would have a salvage value of $1,000. In a prior case, the California court held that copyrights are not subject to the personal property tax.[51] The court held for the County of Los Angeles, stating that the value of intangibles can be included in the valuation of tangible property.

In *District of Columbia* v. *Norwood Studios, Inc.*, the issue was whether the sale of a motion picture produced under contract for television is the sale of personal services or the sale of a product subject to the sales tax.[52]

Norwood argued unsuccessfully that the tangible personal property involved was an inconsequential element and was, therefore, not subject to the sales tax.[53]

The Alabama Supreme Court has held that leased motion picture films constitute tangible personal property for privilege or license tax purposes.[54] The Arkansas Supreme Court held in *American Television Co. v. Hervey*, that a levy of a use tax on videotape material used by television stations pursuant to license agreements is a tax on tangible personal property.[55] That court said:

> We agree with the state that the right to use property cannot be separated from the property itself and the "right" spoken of by appellant would have no value except for the use of the tape or film—the two cannot be separated.[56]

The Michigan Appellate Court held that the master film negatives used to store printed material are tangible property even though the value of the property is in the information that is stored and not in the film itself.[57] In support of its contention that the master negatives were intangible property, Unviersity Microfilms cited a line of cases holding real estate abstract books[58] and computer software[59] to be intangible, arguing that its master negatives are analogous to abstract books and software, because these items are only valuable for the information they contain.

The federal courts have addressed the film tangibility issue from an investment tax credit perspective. In *Walt Disney Productions v. United States* (Disney I), master film negatives, which are used to make film prints, were held to be tangible property eligible for the investment tax credit.[60] The master negatives, which are used to make other products (film prints), were likened to a machine which makes other products.

In *Disney III*, the fact situation was similar, but the issues were somewhat different.[61] In holding that the master film negatives in question were tangible property qualifying for the investment tax credit, the court also held that the investment tax credit taken is not subject to recapture, even though the film prints were used predominantly outside the United States for the period under audit. Treasury Regulation Section 1.48-1(g)(i) provides that property physically located outside the United States during more than 50 percent of the year shall be considered used predominantly outside the United States, which would make the property ineligible for the investment tax credit. However, the master negatives (upon which the investment tax credit was claimed) remained in the United States throughout 1970. Only the exhibition prints left the country, and the investment tax credit was not claimed on them. Therefore, no investment tax credit need be recaptured. The court also held that even though the property in question may be treated as intangible for depreciation purposes, such treatment does not preclude tangible treatment for purposes of the investment tax credit.

Cases Involving the Sale of Information

Stock Exchange Data

In *Dun & Bradstreet* v. *City of New York*, the New York Court of Appeals considered the applicability of a local sales tax law in relation to the rendition of professional services.[62] The taxpayer was in the business of supplying to its subscribers highly confidential information dealing with the financial standing of persons engaged in various businesses. As an incident to this service, each subscriber received for his own personal use a reference book at no extra charge.

In refusing to allow the City of New York to tax the value of this reference book, the court articulated two factors that have since been used by other courts to distinguish tangible personalty from intangibles. First, the subscriber was able to make only a limited use of the books. Under the subscription contracts, title to the books remained in the taxpayer, and the subscriber was expressly forbidden to share the confidential information contained therein with the public. Second, and more important, the physical properties of the reference book were merely incidental to the services performed. As explained by the court:

> The information furnished is of value to the subscribers and for it they pay, but not for the paper upon which the information is conveyed or for the reference books which are only guides to assist in the rendition of appellant's service. One does not think of a telephone company as a seller of books to its subscribers. It renders a service to make that service efficient, it furnishes its subscribers with books containing a list of its subscribers with their call numbers. The paper is a mere incident; the skilled service is that which is required.[63]

The two factors enumerated in this case have been used in software tax cases to argue that software is intangible and, therefore, not subject to tax, since (1) the software license agreement prohibits the licensee to share the program with anyone else; (2) the licensor retains title; and, (3) the physical medium used (cards, tapes, disks, and so forth) is merely incidental to the service performed.[64]

However, magazines have been held to be tangible property, subject to the retailers' occupation tax unless otherwise exempt. The Illinois Supreme Court ruled that:

> The sale of magazines is essentially not different from the sale of a loaf of bread, or an automobile. While it is true that the utility or value of plaintiffs' magazines is in their content and not the paper and ink with which they are printed, the taxability of the transaction is not determined by weighing the value of the intangible properties of the item of sale, such as form, organization, and design, against the value of its tangible properties, such as weight, size, and texture. The test is, where tangible personal property is transferred, as the parties agree occurs in the transaction here involved, whether the transfer is the

substance of the transaction or merely incidental to a service. In selling magazines by subscriptions, plaintiffs act as retailers of tangible personal property and as such are liable for retailer's occupation tax, if not otherwise exempt.[65]

Dun & Bradstreet can be distinguished from *Time, Inc.*, on the basis of ownership and the nature of the information being conveyed. In *Dun & Bradstreet*, the licensee was paying for confidential information that could not easily be obtained elsewhere, and the information obtained could not be conveyed to others. In *Time, Inc.*, the information could easily be obtained from other sources, including the public library, without purchasing the magazine; and ownership changed upon purchase.

In another case, Bunker-Ramo provided stock brokers and security dealers with stock-exchange information electronically for a fee.[66] As part of the agreement, Bunker-Ramo installed tangible personal property to receive the electronic transmissions on the customer's premises at a cost varying between $6,644 and $16,522. Approximately 110 Bunker-Ramo employees were engaged in customer servicing and the reception, editing, transformation, and preparation of raw data that is eventually transmitted to subscribers. Bunker-Ramo employees make frequent visits to subscriber premises to correct errors.

Bunker-Ramo contended that the transmission of this data constitutes a personal service and is, therefore, not subject to the Ohio sales tax. The tax commissioner alleged that such transmissions constitute the sale of tangible personal property subject to the sales tax.

The Ohio Supreme Court held for the tax commissioner. Citing *American District Telegraph Co. v. Porterfield*,[67] *Randall Park Jockey Club v. Peck*,[68] and *Recording Devices, Inc. v. Bowers*,[69] the court stated that Bunker-Ramo's transactions would be considered sales, because they involve the transfer of possession and licenses to use tangible personal property unless the transactions were found to be personal service transactions.

> An examination of the record indicates that the activity which the appellee performs is a completely mechanized service transaction. It is not a personal service transaction in the sense that there are no people engaged in serving directly the subscribers of appellee. This service is rendered automatically by computers, communication lines and reception and display instruments.[70]

While some services rendered are tailored to the personal needs of subscribers, the relatively small number of people required to oversee, maintain, and service the devices on the subscribers' premises indicated to the court that very little personal service was involved.

In *Quotron Systems, Inc. v. Comptroller of the Treasury*, Quotron provided its subscribers with stock-exchange and other information electronically over leased telephone and telegraph lines from its computer in New York.[71] Quotron provided the hardware its customers needed to receive the information. The comptroller contended that Quotron was providing both a service and hardware to its subscribers. Quotron maintained that only a service was provided, and that it was Quotron, not the subscriber, that was using the hardware. The court held that Quotron was not subject to a Maryland use tax on that part of its monthly charges which was attributable to use of the hardware where the hardware had no utility in and of itself to subscribers.

In its *Quotron* decision, the Maryland Supreme Court relied on *Comptroller of the Treasury* v. *Chesapeake & Potomac Telephone Company*, which held that a two-step analysis should be employed when both services and equipment are involved.[72]

First, the overall function must be characterized by the examination of various factors as either a rental or transfer of possession, or a service. Secondly, it must be determined whether that function is subject to a sales tax. In other jurisdictions in which the same or similar questions have been considered, the same analysis has been employed.[73] Courts in other jurisdictions, which similarly have examined the relationship between equipment and services in characterizing an overall function, have applied a third standard.[74] This standard was expressed by the Supreme Court of Illinois in *Snite* v. *Department of Revenue* as follows:

> If the article sold has no value to the purchaser except as a result of services rendered by the vendor, and the transfer of the article to the purchaser is an actual and necessary part of the service rendered, then the vendor is engaged in the business of rendering service and not in the business of selling at retail. If the article sold is the substance of the transaction, and the service rendered is merely incidental to and an inseparable part of the transfer to the purchaser of the article sold, then the vendor is engaged in the business of selling at retail, and the tax which he pays for the privilege of engaging in such business is measured by the price which the purchaser pays for the article and the service incident thereto.[75]

Credit Information

In *Credit Bureau of Miami County, Inc.* v. *Collins*, the taxpayer provided credit information to customers both orally and in written form.[76] The Ohio Supreme Court held that, in cases where information was transferred in written form, the tangible property conveyed was an inconsequential element in the transaction, and that the true object of the transaction was not the acquisition of the taxpayer's property, but rather the services the taxpayer provided.[77]

Mailing Lists

In *Fingerhut Products Company* v. *Commissioner of Revenue*, a direct mail merchandiser of a wide range of products purchased mailing lists from a broker.⁷⁸ For these labels, Fingerhut paid a rental fee of $17.50 to $25 per 1,000 names. The value of the tangible material upon which the names and addresses are printed is approximately 80 cents per 1,000.

The commissioner assessed a tax deficiency on the rental of these lists, asserting that the lists constituted tangible personal property. Fingerhut contended that the essence of what it received from the brokers was not a physical list of names, but rather a service which supplied highly sophisticated advertising information which was an intangible commodity.

In its unsuccessful argument, Fingerhut maintained that its procurement and use of the mailing lists supplied by its brokers satisfies both of the criteria established in *Dun & Bradstreet* v. *City of New York*, which held that where the subscriber is able to make only limited use of the property and where the value of the physical property is incidental compared to the value of the service, the transaction will be viewed as the purchase of an intangible service rather than a tangible product.⁷⁹ In holding the labels to be tangible, the court said:

> We feel that the use of the Cheshire tapes, gummed labels . . . is a use of the tangible property of the medium distinct . . . in that the tapes and labels are physically separated and attached to the envelopes. In such a case, the physical manifestation of the property is itself used—not merely the intangible information.⁸⁰

In *Spencer Gifts, Inc.* v. *Director, Division of Taxation*, the opposite conclusion was reached.⁸¹ Spencer extracted the mailing list information from a computer tape, which was then promptly returned to the vendor. The value of the information acquired far exceeded the value of the tape, which was returned. In holding that the leasing of computer information is not the leasing of tangible personal property, the court distinguished *Spencer* from *Fingerhut*. In *Fingerhut*, the physical manifestation of the property itself (tapes and labels) was used, whereas in *Spencer* the information was received in incorporeal form. In a more recent case, the New York court held that the purchase of mailing lists obtained by computer tape constitute the purchase of information rather than tangible personal property.⁸² However, the purchase of information is a taxable event in New York.⁸³

Artwork

Some courts have made an analogy of software and certain artwork, since the value of both is attributable primarily to the labor involved and not the tangible property upon which the results of the labor are recorded.⁸⁴ In *Washington Times-Herald, Inc.* v. *District of Columbia*, the newspaper purchased the right to reproduce cartoons from the artist.⁸⁵ These cartoons were transferred to the newspaper and were physically embodied in mats which were then used to reproduce the cartoons in the newspaper. In that case, the court held that what the newspaper had purchased was the right to reproduce the cartoons, and not the material upon which the cartoons were impressed.

> The price was paid for the artists' work, i.e., for the right to reproduce the impressions on the mats—not for the mats themselves. The newspaper bought the creation of the artist—not the material on which it was impressed—and the right to reproduce it. Without that right, the comic strips mats would be entirely worthless.[86]

A similar result was reached by the Florida court in *Southern Bell Telephone and Telegraph Company* v. *Department of Revenue*, where it was held that the sale of artwork that ultimately appears in the telephone book yellow pages constitutes the sale of a service rather than tangible personal property.[87] The court reached its decision after considering the following factors:

1. Whether or not the property to be transferred as a result of the transaction is already in existence or whether it is produced in the course of the services rendered.
2. The value of the individual effort involved in the transaction as compared to the value of the property transferred.
3. Whether or not it is essential to the transaction that the specific tangible personal property is created.[88]

Cases Involving the Uniform Commercial Code

The UCC has different rules for goods and services. If software is classified as goods, it may be classified as tangible property in some states, thereby making the sale of software a taxable event. If classified as a service, the transaction may escape tax. The UCC defines goods as:

> [A]ll things (including specially manufactured goods) which are movable at the time of identification to the contract for sale other than the money in which the price is to be paid.[89]

Helvey v. *Wabash County REMC* addressed the issue of whether electrical energy is a good or a service.[90] In order to be a good under the UCC, the property in question must be (1) a thing; (2) existing; and, (3) movable, with (2) and ((3) existing simultaneously. The court held that electricity qualifies in each respect.

Although *Helvey* was concerned with whether the six year statute of limitations (for sale of a service) or the four year statute (sale of a good) applied, the fact that electrical energy was classified as a good rather than a service is significant, because software is sometimes transferred over telephone lines, and such transfers could be construed as being the transfer of tangible personal property subject to sales and use taxation, although several courts have suggested that a transfer of software over telephone lines is not a taxable event.[91]

In *Carl Beasley Ford, Inc. v. Burroughs Corporation*, the court held that the purchase of bundled hardware and software constitutes the purchase of a good rather than a service.[92] The acquisition did not function properly due to faulty programming, and Beasley sued for recovery of the purchase price under the UCC. The hardware was virtually useless without the software.

In *F&M Schaefer Corporation v. Electronic Data Systems Corporation*, the court held software to be tangible for replevin purposes.[93] In another case decided at about the same time as *F & M Schaefer*, the New York court held that the purchase of a "turn-key" system involving both hardware and software constituted the sale of a good, so that the UCC's four year statute of limitations for breach of contract applies, rather than the six year statute for breach involving a service.[94] The *Triangle* court based its reasoning on *North American Leisure Corp. v. A & B Duplicators, Ltd.*, which held that a contract is for a service rather than sale when service predominates, and the sale of items is incidental.[95] In *Triangle*, the precise converse was true. The essence of the contract was for the sale of goods. While certain services by Honeywell were contemplated, the contract was primarily one for the sale of goods.[96]

Chatlos Systems, Inc. v. National Cash Register Corporation, Inc., also involved a breach of contract action.[97] Chatlos purchased a computer system involving both hardware and software components from NCR. The system did not function as promised, and Chatlos brought an action for breach of warranty. The court held the property in question to be a tangible good, and that the UCC rather than common law contract law applied. The transaction was for the sale of goods notwithstanding the incidental service aspects and the lease arrangement.[98] On appeal, both parties conceded the applicability of the UCC.

Cases Involving Data Processing Service Bureaus

Data processing service bureaus perform functions that are not always easy to classify as falling neatly and exclusively into either the product or service category. In an early series of Ohio cases,[99] the Ohio Supreme Court quoted an even earlier Arizona case, which set forth the following possibilities regarding mixed sales of services and property:

(1) The service is the main item sold, and the property sold is incidental thereto and not separately charged (not a taxable sale as a sale of services).

(2) The services and property sold can be readily separated (one tax exempt and the other taxable).

(3) The service sold is incidental to the property and not separately charged (taxable in gross).[100]

The Arizona court, recognizing that the category into which a vendor falls is a question of fact to be determined in light of all the evidence, stated that:

> When there is a fixed and ascertainable relationship between the value of the article and the value of the service rendered in connection therewith so that both may be separately stated, then the vendor is engaged in both selling at retail and furnishing services and is subject to the tax as to one and tax exempt as to the other. Where the property and the services are distinct and each is a consequential element capable of ready separation, it cannot be said one is an inconsequential element within the exemption provided by the statute. See *Rice* v. *Evatt*, 144 Ohio St. 483, 59 N.E.2d 927, 157 A.L.R. 572 (1945).[101]

In *Accountants Computer Services*, raw data was received from customers in the form of punch paper tapes or adding machine tapes upon which the customer's debits and credits are recorded. Accountants then processed the information by machine and furnished individual clients with printouts that were used by the customer to draft financial statements, and so forth. Data were sorted, classified, and rearranged by Accountants machine. The court held that this process results in the sale of a product rather than a service and, as such, is subject to the Ohio sales tax.

Central Data Systems provided clients with data processing, key punching, systems design and programming, and contract consulting. In this case, the court determined that what was being sold was a service rather than a product. *Central* can be distinguished from *Accountants* because, in *Central*, the company's professional workers applied "thinking" as well as mechanical processing. It was the analysis and thinking skills of Central employees that was being sold; the data processing machinery and related printouts were merely used by Central personnel to assist them in rendering their personal service. Because the personal service was the main item contracted for, and the resulting printed matter constituted an inconsequential element for which no separate charge was made, the court held that the sale of the tangible personal property was not subject to taxation.

In *Jergens*, the company contracted with A. C. Nielsen Company, a market research organization. Nielsen was to compile statistical data as well as to provide analysis and interpretation of data, and to assist management in making marketing decisions based on the data provided. As an integral part of the service furnished, Nielsen assigned account executives to Jergens' account whose duty it was to analyze, interpret, and present to Jergens' management the information developed by Nielsen in a meaningful and useful manner.

The Andrew Jergens Company case represents an even clearer example of a transaction involving the sale of a service rather than a product. The A. C. Nielsen Company was hired to gather, analyze, and interpret data and to assist AJC's management in making marketing decisions. It was clearly the personal service of Nielsen and its staff that was contracted for; the tangible personal property that was transferred for communication purposes was an inconsequential element without separate charge. The entire transaction is exempt from the Ohio sales tax.

In its reasoning, the court cited several other Ohio cases where the sales tax was assessed on the entire consideration paid in transactions that involved insignificant and inconsequential amounts of personal services.[102] No reduction was made for the portion of the consideration that was attributable to personal services.

The rationale for not separating the inconsequential amount attributable to personal services from the amount attributable to tangible personal property is that: (1) nearly all transactions are, of necessity, mixed transactions involving at least a slight degree of personal service and (2) where this degree of personal service is of insignificant consequence, both the practical problem of attributing to such service a percentage of the entire consideration paid, and the insignificant effect it would have on the amount paid in taxes, make such a distinction unreasonable and unnecessary.

Two years after the above three cases were decided, the Ohio Supreme Court was once again called upon to decide a computer service bureau case. In *Citizens Financial Corp.* v. *Kosydar*, Citizens provided both off-line and on-line services to the thrift industry.[103]

In the off-line method, the tellers at the customer savings and loan manually record the daily deposits and withdrawals, and the recorded transactions are daily delivered to the taxpayer, where the information is converted by the computer into "computer legible media." Subsequently, the taxpayer delivers to the customer a "hard-copy printout" which provides the customer with an accounting journal of daily transactions, thus updating the individual account records. A fee is charged, based on the number of such accounts each customer maintains in the computer.

The on-line method consists of teller use of terminals which are located at the tellers' windows. Passbooks are placed in the terminals and by means of depression of appropriate keys, the transaction (deposit, withdrawal, or loan payment) is transmitted via telephone lines to taxpayer's computers. The computers then make the programmed calculation, printing the transaction on both the customer's passbook and upon a printout at the terminal. Subsequently, a hard copy journal of transactions is delivered by taxpayer to the customer. A fee is charged, as in the off-line method.

The court held both the on-line and off-line transactions to be taxable and not within the personal service exemption. As in *Accountants Computer Services, Inc.* v. *Kosydar*, the true object of the transaction was held to be the property produced, for example, the "hard-copy printouts" rather than a service.[104] In its decision, the *Citizens* court used the criteria as enunciated in *Koch* v. *Kosydar* to determine whether a service transaction existed.[105]

In his dissent in *Citizens*, Justice Paul W. Brown, pointing to his dissent in *United States Shoe Corp.* v. *Kosydar*, stated that the personal service exception must be seriously distorted before it can be construed to impose a tax upon a service transaction.[106] He also cited Appendix 2 - 3.2d of 1 Bigelow, Computer Law Service (1975), *State Sales and Use Taxes*, which indicates that similar transactions would be exempt from the sales tax had they occurred in Connecticut, Louisiana, New York, Texas, Virginia, Washington, or Wisconsin.

In a Florida case, the Department of Revenue enacted a rule construing computer software (punched cards, paper tapes, and typed sheets) to be tangible personal property and subject to the sales tax.[107] Nova filed a petition challenging the validity of the rule. The administrative hearing officer in that case found that when computer software is sold it is the computer information which is transferred, and that the magnetic tapes or punch cards which contain the information are only the means or method of transmitting it from the originator to the user. It was further determined that the tangible property (for example, punch cards) involved in the process was an inconsequential element for which no separate charges were made, the consequential element being intangible property (computer information) which was not subject to the sales tax on tangible personal property. The conclusion was that Nova and other similar corporations were selling services to their customers which were exempt from the sales tax.

In *Bullock* v. *Statistical Tabulating Corporation*, customers brought in raw data, for example, business records and invoices, which Statistical Tabulating Corporation then translated into computer-readable code and transferred onto cards that can be read by the customer's computer.[108] Once read, the cards have no further use. There is no separate charge to the customers for the cards.

In holding that the transactions in question constitute the sale of services rather than tangible personal property, the Texas court used the same test it used in *Williams and Lee Scouting Service, Inc.* v. *Calvert*, which stated that if the object or the essence of the sale is not tangible personal property but intangible property, then the transaction is not taxable under any definition of "sale."[109]

In *Miami Citizens National Bank & Trust Company* v. *Lindley*, a bank performed data processing for other banks and furnished its customers with a series of reports which reveal considerable information for use by the correspondent bank in making informed management decisions for future operations.[110] The sales tax was assessed only on charges for computer printouts and not for programming time.

In holding the entire transaction to be taxable, the court reasoned that the true object of the transactions is the receipt of the printed form which contains the computer organized data.[111]

Cases Involving the Sale of Software

Cases dealing specifically with the sale of computer software are of relatively recent origin. Prior to June, 1969, when IBM began stating separate prices for its software, the software was acquired in conjunction with the hardware.[112] Shortly after this change in policy, state taxing commissions began to tax software as if it were tangible property. Soon, the issue of tangibility began to be settled in court.

The first case to address the software tangibility issue directly was *District of Columbia* v. *Universal Computer Associates*.[113] In this case, Universal purchased hardware and software from IBM. One set of punched cards was a special tax program developed jointly by Universal and IBM and owned outright by Universal. The other set of cards was a standard set used to run the computer.

The court ruled that the software portion of the purchase was intangible and was not subject to the personal property tax, and that the portion representing hardware was tangible and subject to the tax. The $290,000 purchase price was allocated 50 percent to the hardware and 50 percent to the software.

Since no previously decided case was directly on point, other cases dealing with the sales versus service issue were examined. The material of the punched cards themselves is of insignificant value. It was the knowledge contained in the cards that gave them value, and knowledge is intangible. The court likened computer software to the cartoon mats involved in *Washington Times-Herald* v. *District of Columbia*, where it was held that cartoon mats which were sold by publishing syndicates to individual newspapers were not tangible personal property subject to the District of Columbia sales tax.[114]

In *Universal*, the court is of the opinion that the knowledge stored on computer cards, tapes, or disks is even more demonstrably intangible intellectual property than the right to reproduce from the cartoonist's drawings involved in *Washington Times-Herald*.

Universal is distinguished from *District of Columbia* v. *Norwood Studios, Inc.*, which involved the transfer of films where the producer of the films retained no interest in them and imposed no restriction on their use.[115] The films became the property of the purchasers without qualification.

Because *Universal Computer Associates* was the first case to address the issue of software tangiblity, it has been cited by many subsequent cases.

The following year, the California court addressed the tangibility issue. In *County of Sacramento* v. *Assessment Appeals Board*, data processing equipment and systems were furnished on a conditional sales basis to the State of California.[116] The tax assessor, in assessing the sales tax liability, valued the property at the full contract price. The equipment and systems in question consisted of both hardware and software components.

The court held that the tax assessor was in error when he valued the property at full contract price. The portion of the contract price attributable to software represents intangible property not subject to the sales tax.

In another early case, Greyhound Computer Corporation purchased several computer systems where the price of the hardware and software were not separately stated.[117] Maryland treated the cost of the software as inseparable from that of the hardware and based its property tax assessment on aggregate purchase price, less depreciation, without allocating the cost of the software package between tangible property acquired and services to be rendered. The court held that it was an error not to allocate the purchase price between the tangible and intangible components, and remanded the case for further proceedings.[118]

In 1976, the tangibility issue was decided in Tennessee, in the frequently cited case of *Commerce Union Bank* v. *Tidwell*.[119] In this case, Commerce Union Bank purchased software for use in its business. The commissioner of revenue (Tidwell) assessed a tax deficiency, alleging that the transfer was one of tangible personal property subject to the Tennessee sales tax.

The band alleged that while the intellectual processes may be embodied in tangible and physical material, such as punch cards and magnetic tapes, the logic or intelligence of the program is an intangible property right, and it is this intangible property right which is acquired when computer software is purchased or leased.

Tidwell viewed the purchase of software as analogous to the purchase of a phonograph record or the purchase or lease of a motion picture film. He argued that the present case is governed by *Crescent Amusement Co.* v. *Carson*, where a tax was levied on the rental of motion picture films.[120]

In holding software to be intangible, the court rejected Tidwell's argument that software is similar to a motion picture film. Whereas, without a film there would be no movie, magnetic tapes and cards are not a crucial element of software. The whole of computer software could be transmitted orally or electronically without any tangible manifestations of transmission. Whereas, a product is created in the case of a film or phonograph record, there is no product in the case of software. What is created and sold is information, and the magnetic tapes which contain this information are only a method of transmitting these intellectual creations from the original to the user. It is merely incidental that these intangibles are transmitted by way of a tangible reel of tape that is not even retained by the user. Furthermore, Tennessee did not attempt to tax computer programs purchased by the bank which were transmitted to its computers from outside the state by way of telephone lines. That method was deemed to constitute the purchase of intangible personal property. The principle is the same; only the method of transmitting the information is different.

Another difference between software and phonograph records is the fact that, when the information is transferred from the tape to the computer, the tape is no longer of any value to the user; and it is not retained in the possession of the user. The information on the tape, unlike the phonograph record, is not complete and ready to be used at the time of its purchase. It must be translated into a language understood by the computer. Once this information has been translated and introduced into the computer and the tapes returned or the punch cards destroyed, what actually remains in the computer is intangible knowledge; this is what was purchased, not the magnetic tapes or the punch cards.[121]

Transfer of tangible personal property under these circumstances is merely incidental to the purchase of the intangible knowledge and information stored on the tapes.[122]

The year after *Commerce Union Bank* v. *Tidwell* was decided in Tennessee, the Alabama Supreme Court reached a similar conclusion in a case having a similar fact pattern. In *State of Alabama* v. *Central Computer Services, Inc.*, Central Computer Services, Inc. licensed certain software programs for a 99-year term.[123] Upon receipt of the software, Central extracted the information contained on the magnetic tapes and punched cards and transferred the programs to magnetic disks. The tapes were then returned to the lessor, and the cards were thrown away. The Alabama State Department of Revenue assessed a use tax of $13,519.91 against Central for its purchase of the programs. Central alleged the programs were intangible property and, therefore, not subject to the use tax.

In holding for Central, the court ruled that what was purchased by Central was the information or knowledge which went into the development of the eight programs and not the magnetic tapes and punched cards themselves. The magnetic tapes and punched cards were merely the means by which this information or knowledge was transferred.

The state contended that the magnetic tapes and punched cards are a necessary, integral part of the computer program and that because these items are tangible, there was a purchase of taxable tangible personal property by Central.

In its argument, the state cited *Boswell* v. *Paramount Television Sales, Inc.*[124] In that case, the court held that the leasing of movie films and tapes by Paramount to television stations in Alabama involved the leasing of tangible personal property rather than an intangible right to publish as Paramount argued.

The court in *Central* distinguished the magnetic tapes and punched cards from the movie films. In *Boswell*, the court noted that the right to publish or broadcast the motion picture was physically inseparable from the movie film itself. The physical presence of the movie film is essential to broadcasting the intangible artistic efforts of the actors.

However, in *Central*, the physical presence of magnetic tapes and punched cards is not essential to the transmittal of the desired information from its creator to Central. This information can also be telephoned to the computer or brought into Alabama in the mind of an employee of the lessor.

In its summary, the court said that:

> [W]e find in the present case that there is an incidental physical commingling of the intangible information sought by Central Computer Services and the tangible magnetic tapes and punched cards themselves. We therefore hold that the essence of this transaction was the purchase of nontaxable intangible information.[125]

Texas, which first addressed the software tax issue in 1977 in *Bullock* v. *Statistical Tabulating Corp.*,[126] addressed the issue a second time in 1979 in *First National Bank of Fort Worth* v. *Bullock*.[127] In the 1979 case, the bank purchased several standardized or canned programs which enabled its computer to perform deposit and lending functions and process general accounting. The software was contained on magnetic tapes, but the information could have been transmitted by keypunch cards, telephone, or various other methods.

The Texas law places a tax on a sale of tangible personal property. Tangible personal property is defined as "personal property which may be seen, weighed, measured, felt, or touched, or which is in any other manner perceptible to the senses."[128] To determine whether a sale is of tangible or intangible property, the courts apply the "essence of the transaction" test.[129] If the object or essence of the sale is intangible property, then the transaction is not taxable. An important factor to be considered in arriving at this determination is the fact that the desired information could have been transferred in several different ways.[130]

In *Statistical Tabulating*, the court held that processed data contained in a coded computer card was an intangible and not taxable. In *Williams and Lee Scouting*, statistical data on oil and gas well production was compiled and mailed to subscribers in printed reports each week. The sale was not taxed. The purchasers in both *Williams and Lee Scouting* and *Statistical Tabulating* were desirous of something beyond the tangible object involved in the transaction. Unlike a phonograph record or filmstrip when the information on the tape, in the present case, is transferred to the computer, the tape is no longer of any value or importance to the user.[131]

Bullock contended that this case is distinguishable from *Statistical Tabulating* in that the software in the latter case was customized, because it was developed specially for the purchaser. The tapes in the present case are canned programs, since they are standard items sold to numerous customers with only slight modifications to conform to each purchaser's use. The service characteristic is present only with customized programs, according to Bullock.

The court did not agree with Bullock's argument that only customized programs should be exempt from the sales tax. The test in each case is not whether the product is customized or canned, but whether the object of the sale is tangible personal property.[132] In *Williams and Lee Scouting*, the weekly report of oil and gas data was a canned publication in that the same information was mailed to many subscribers.

The Texas court held that the programs in question were intangible and not subject to the sales tax.

Two years after the *First National Bank of Fort Worth* v. *Bullock* was decided in Texas, the Illinois Supreme Court heard a similar case and reached the same conclusion as the Texas court. In *First National Bank of Springfield* v. *Department of Revenue*, the issue was whether the sale of applicational programs (as opposed to operational programs) constitutes the sale of tangible personal property subject to the Illinois use tax, where the data is contained on magnetic tape.[133] As was the case in *Fort Worth*, the bank in *Springfield* purchased computer programs that were delivered on magnetic tape, although other means of delivery were also possible.

Upon delivery, the information was removed from the tapes and stored elsewhere, at which point the tapes could either be used again or discarded.

The bank contended that the magnetic tapes in question here constituted intangible personal property, because they were, in essence, merely a means of conveying programming instructions and that software primarily represents intangible services and not tangible goods. The department, on the contrary, contended that the physical qualities of the tapes predominate over the information contained on them. The department compared the tapes to films, phonograph records, and books. All three examples, the department argued, represent the physical manifestation of intangible ideas and artistic achievement, yet all three are taxable as tangible personal property.[134]

The Illinois court held that the software in question was intangible. The Illinois court previously held that where a service of skill was rendered in the manufacture of a special milling machine for the particular and exclusive use of a purchaser, the sale of the product was not taxable where it was merely incidental to the service.[135] The instant case is of a similar vein. The plaintiff bank purchased, in substance, the means of programming its computer so that it could perform functions the bank needed to have performed. The bank did not desire to spend the money or time to formulate the programs through its own data processing staff. Therefore, it purchased instruction programs from other sources. It simply happened that, for the sake of convenience and easy handling, the programs were recorded on magnetic tapes. The tapes were certainly not the only medium through which the information could be transferred. In this way, the tapes differ from a movie film, a phonograph record, or a book, whereby the media used are the only practicable ways of preserving those articles.

Thus, while those articles and the tapes are similar in that they physically represent the transfer of ideas or artistic processes, a more significant distinction is that those articles are inseparable from the ideas or processes, whereas computer programs are separable from the tapes. Not only may software information be conveyed any number of ways, but it may even be copied off of the tapes and stored, using another medium. In short, it is not the tapes which are the substance of the transaction, it is the information.[136]

The court held that the sale of computer software in this instance is, in substance, the transfer of intangible personal property and, as such, is not taxable under the Illinois Use Tax Act.[137]

Soon after the *First National Bank of Springfield* case was decided in Illinois, a case having a similar fact pattern was heard across the border in Missouri. In *James* v. *TRES Computer Service, Inc.*, the issue was whether the sale of canned software is a taxable event.[138] In holding software to be intangible and not subject to the Missouri use tax, the court based its decision on the decisions reached in Alabama, Tennessee, Texas, Illinois, the District of Columbia, and Wisconsin.[139]

1983 — A Turning Point or an Aberration?

A long line of cases in a number of states, going back as far as 1972, have ruled almost uniformly that software is intangible for state sales, use, and property tax purposes. The "knowledge" rationale has been used, as have the "essence of the transaction" and several other tests. Software has been compared to and distinguished from films, records, and books, all of which have been held to be tangible.

In 1983, two court cases decided one day apart, have flown in the face of this long line of precedent. In *Comptroller of the Treasury* v. *Equitable Trust Company*, the issue was whether the purchase of a canned or off-the-shelf program on magnetic tape constitutes a transaction upon which sales tax can be assessed.[140]

Equitable entered into several license agreements whereby it obtained the nontransferable and nonexclusive right to use several programs in perpetuity. Legal title remained with the licensor.

The comptroller alleged that these transactions constitute transactions involving tangible personal property—namely, magnetic tapes which had been enhanced in value by the copies of the programs coded thereon and are subject to sales tax. In its *amicus* brief, the Data Processing Management Association (DPMA) contended that the transactions were licenses to use the programs, and that such licenses are a form of intangible property. Equitable contended that the predominant purpose or essence of the transaction governs classification of the sale as involving either tangible or intangible property. In the transfer of computer programs via magnetic tape, the purpose is to obtain the program, an intangible, and not the tangible tape. In taking this position, Equitable is supported by the overwhelming numerical majority of reported cases applying tax statutes restricted to tangible personal property.

In holding for the comptroller, the court held that Equitable acquired tangible personal property—namely, magnetic tapes which had been enhanced in value by the copies of the programs coded thereon. The licenses do not grant intangible rights from the proprietors to Equitable but simply erect contractual limitations on the use which Equitable might otherwise make of the statutorily unprotected program copies it acquired.[141]

Equitable's principal argument is that the court should conceptually sever the program copy contained on the magnetic tape from the tangible tape itself. The argument is that the transaction should be viewed as operating on two levels—one the transfer of intangible knowledge or information and, the other, the delivery of a tangible tape. To have a scalpel for this legal surgery, it would be necessary to adopt as part of Maryland sales tax law a principle that the buyer's predominant purpose for a transaction controls the classification of the acquisition as either tangible or intangible.

Quotron Systems v. *Comptroller* recognized a predominant purpose test as one of several factors in determining use tax applicability to the type of transaction presented there.[142] That taxpayer undertook concurrently to render two types of interrelated performances. One was to maintain and continuously to update a computerized data bank of economic information, such as the selling prices of securities, which its customers could randomly access through remote terminals. The other was to install Quotron-owned hardware, including the remote terminals, on customers' premises for their use in requesting and receiving electronic transmissions of the economic data. In *Quotron*, the court held that the first analytical step was to characterize the performance as a single, overall function, either rental of equipment or the provision of services.[143] The dominant purpose was to obtain services and not to rent hardware. Based on that factor, on the taxpayer's retention of control over the hardware, and on the fact that Quotron's hardware could not be obtained without subscribing to the service, the court concluded that the transaction was the provision of services.[144] This approach is quite similar to that which the court used to determine whether a contract of sale is one for goods or for services under Article 2 of the UCC, where the performance involves both.[145]

The rule of *Quotron* has been implicitly applied in *Equitable* on an aspect which is not disputed by Equitable. In addition to providing program copies on tape, each licensor agreed to furnish certain installation services. One licensor also contracted to furnish a limited amount of training within the fixed contract price.

The "dominant purpose" test of whether the property in question is being purchased for its own sake or for the (intangible) information contained therein can also be applied, by analogy, to books, motion picture films, video-display discs, phonorecords and music tapes. In sales of these items, the purchaser's dominant purpose ordinarily is to obtain the knowledge, information, or data thereby conveyed. While the book is in human readable form, the other media are machine readable. A purchase of any of these information conveying media is within the imposition of the sales tax as tangible personal property. Such transactions escape taxation only if there is an applicable statutory exclusion or exemption. These analogies, however, have been argued to other courts which have held that tape copies of programs are intangible.

The court in *Equitable* rejected the reasoning of the long line of cases that hold taped copies to be intangible because of alleged misconceptions in the technological underpinnings of these decisions, and because of the apparent departures in reasoning from that usually applied in sales tax cases. Secondly, there was a substantial question whether the decision that set the course for the line of program cases, *District of Columbia* v. *Universal Computer Associates, Inc.*, is consistent with Maryland law.[146]

Furthermore, a tape containing a copy of a canned program does not lose its tangible character, because its content is a reproduction of the product of intellectual effort, just as the phonograph record does not become intangible, because it is a reproduction of the product of artistic effort. The price paid for a copy of a canned program reflects the cost of developing the program which the proprietor hopes to recover, with profit, by spreading the cost among its customers. Simply because the canned program on tape is much more expensive than the typical phonorecord, the program tape is not any less tangible.

The court stated that Equitable's intangibility argument would have merit if the direct input by keyboard, without documentation or the electronic transmission, without documentation is the form of transaction under consideration. But, because a taxable transaction might have been structured in a nontaxable form, it does not thereby become nontaxable.[147]

Finally, Equitable argues that a purchased program "can be and was in fact severed and exists apart from the tangible transfer medium. . . ." However, the copy delivered to Equitable does not become severed in any physical sense from the tape when the tape is used to structure computer memory.

The *Equitable* court did not discern any legally significant difference for sales tax purposes between the canned computer program on magnetic tape and music on a phonograph record. As stated in the *National Commission on New Technological Uses of Copyrighted Works*, Final Report at 10 (1978): "Both recorded music and computer programs are sets of information in a form which, when passed over a magnetized head, cause minute currents to flow in such a way that desired physical work is accomplished." In the case of the phonograph record, the sales tax statute in Maryland has never been viewed as conceptually severing the copy of the performance from the tangible carrier. The court concluded that the statute does not sever copies of computer programs from the tangible carriers employed in the subject sales.

The day after the *Equitable* case was decided in Maryland, the Vermont court issued its ruling on *Chittenden Trust Company* v. *King*.[148] In this case, the Department of Taxes assessed a compensating use tax of $471 against the Chittenden Trust Company for the purchase of a canned software tape valued at $15,700. The department classified the tape as tangible personal property, subject to taxation. The bank contended the tape was intangible and, therefore, exempt from the tax.

The bank purchased the program in the form of a magnetic tape. The programming information could have been carried using several other means, including punch cards, telephone lines, and personal programming. The 15-20 years needed to develop the off-the-shelf program accounts for almost its total value, since a blank magnetic tape may be purchased for approximately $15. Once the information is transferred into the computer's memory, the tape is of negligible value to the bank, and may be reused, destroyed, or returned to its original distributor.

The court held for the department. The computer tape was held to be tangible personal property and its sale is subject to taxation. In 32 V.S.A. Sec. 970(7), tangible personal property is defined as:

> [P]ersonal property which may be seen, weighed, measured, felt, touched or in any other manner perceived by the senses and shall include fuel and electricity, but shall not include rights and credits, insurance policies, bills of exchange, stocks and bonds, and similar evidences of indebtedness or ownership.

In holding that the computer tape was tangible personal property, the court noted that the tape could be seen, weighed, measured, and touched and is not a right or credit. The court rejected the bank's contention that the "focus of the transaction" was the transfer of intangible knowledge and information, rather than the tangible magnetic tape, because the purchase of an off-the-shelf program does not involve the sale of personal services, but rather the sale of tangible personal property.

The court also rejected the bank's attempts to distinguish a computer program tape from other taxable personal property such as films, videotapes, books, cassettes, and records. The reasoning was that in each, their value lies in their respective abilities to store and later display or transmit their contents, and a computer software tape is no different.

In the final page of its decision, the court stated that:

> It may well be that the Bank could have procured, by way of telephone or personal service, the same programming information so as to avoid a use tax. To base the tax consequences of a transaction on how it could have been structured "would require rejection of the established tax principle that a transaction is to be given its tax effect in accordance with what actually occurred and

not in accordance with what might have occurred." *Commissioner* v. *National Alfalfa Dehydrating & Milling Co.*, 417 U.S. 134, 148 (1974). This we will not do. The Bank must accept the consequences of its choice to purchase the program in the form of a tape.

It will take some time to determine whether the decisions in *Equitable*, *Citizens*, and *Chittenden* are aberrations or the beginning of a trend. Many state legislatures have statutes that classify canned and custom software either as tangible or intangible, but several states have not yet addressed the tangibility issue as it relates to software. As technology advances, some states may reexamine their position on software, and some decisions may be influenced by *Equitable, Citizens*, and *Chittenden*. Only time will tell.

Notes to Chapters

Chapter 1

[1] The decision to "unbundle" was made in part for antitrust reasons. See Schmedel, "IBM Discloses Plan for Separating Its Computer and Services Prices," *The Wall Street Journal*, June 24, 1969, p. 38; Goetz, "When IBM Unbundled," *Computerworld*, December 31, 1979/January 7, 1980, p. 35; Goetz, "Unbundling: Will 80's Repeat the 60's?," *Computerworld*, April 14, 1980, p. 33; John G. Martin, "The Revolt Against the Property Tax on Software: An Unnecessary Conflict Growing out of Unbundling," *Suffolk University Law Review* 9 (Fall 1974), p. 124.

[2] Rev. Proc. 69-21, 1969-2 C.B. 303.

[3] Section 174 of the Internal Revenue Code permits expensing or amortization of research and development costs at the taxpayer's option.

[4] Rev. Rul. 71-177, 1971-1 C.B. 5.

[5] Rev. Rul. 71-248, 1971-1 C.B. 55.

[6] See "Software Industry Analysis" in *Computer Yearbook* (Saint Clair Shores, Mich.: Scholarly Press, 1972), p. 98.

[7] *American National Dictionary for Information Processing*, American Standards Committee, X3, Technical Report 1-77.

[8] Federal Information Processing Standards Publication 11-1, September 30, 1977.

[9] Rev. Proc. 69-21, 1969-2 C.B. 303.

[10] *Commerce Union Bank* v. *Tidwell*, 538 S.W.2d 405, 406 (Tenn. 1976); see also, *Greyhound Computer Corp.* v. *State Department of Assessments and Taxation*, 271 Md. 674, 320 A.2d 52 (1974).

[11] John W. Bryant and Lance R. Mather, "Property Taxation of Computer Software," *New York Law Forum* 18 (1972), pp. 62, 69.

[12] Rev. Rul. 71-177, 1971-1 C.B. 5.

[13] *Texas Instruments, Inc.* v. *United States*, 407 F.Supp. 1326 (N.D. Tex. 1976), *rev'd.* 551 F.2d 599, 39 AFTR2d 77-1383 (5th Cir. 1977).

[14] *Bullock* v. *Statistical Tabulating Corp.*, 549 S.W.2d 166 (Texas 1977); *Commerce Union Bank* v. *Tidwell*, 538 S.W.2d 405 (Tenn. 1976); *County of Sacramento* v. *Assessment Appeals Board*, 32 Cal. App.3d 654, 108 Cal. Rptr. 434 (1973); *First National Bank of Fort Worth* v. *Bullock*, 584 S.W.2d 548 (Tex. Civ. App. 1979); *Janesville Data Center, Inc.* v. *Wisconsin Department of Revenue*, 84 Wis.2d 341, 267 N.W.2d 656 (1978).

[15] *First National Bank of Springfield* v. *Department of Revenue*, 85 Ill.2d 84, 421 N.E.2d 175 (1981); *James* v. *Tres Computer Systems, Inc.*, 642 S.W.2d 347 (Mo. 1982); *Quotron Systems* v. *Comptroller*, 287 Md. 178, 411 A.2d 439 (1980); *State of Alabama* v. *Central Computer Services, Inc.*, 349 So.2d 1160 (1977).

¹⁶*District of Columbia* V. *Universal Computer Associates, Inc.*, 465 F.2d 615 (D.C. Cir. 1972); *Greyhound Computer Corporation* v. *State Department of Assessments and Taxation*, 271 Md. 674, 320 A.2d 52 (1974); *Honeywell Information Systems, Inc.* v. *Maricopa County*, 118 Ariz. 171, 575 P.2d 801 (1978).

¹⁷*Comptroller of the Treasury* v. *Equitable Trust Company* 464 A.2d 248 (Md. 1983), held that the sale of software constitutes the sale of tangible personal property subject to the Maryland sales tax. *Chittenden Trust Company* v. *King* 465 A.2d 1100 (Vt. 1983), held that software is tangible and subject to the Vermont use tax. Also see *Citizens and Southern Systems, Inc.* v. *South Carolina Tax Commission*, South Carolina Supreme Court Opinion No. 22024 (January 10, 1984).

¹⁸*Carl Beasley Ford, Inc.* v. *Burroughs Corporation*, 361 F. Supp. 325 (E.D. Pa. 1973), *aff'd*. 493 F.2d 1400 (3d Cir. 1974); *Chatlos Systems, Inc.* v. *National Cash Register Corporation*, 479 F. Supp. 738 (D.N.J. 1979), 635 F.2d 1081 (1980); *Triangle Underwriters, Inc.* v. *Honeywell, Inc.*, 457 F. Supp. 765 (E.D. N.Y. 1978), *rev'd on other grounds*, 604 F.2d 737 (2d Cir. 1979).

¹⁹*F & M Schaefer Corp.* v. *Electronic Data Systems Corp.*, 430 F. Supp. 988 (S.D.N.Y. 1977), *aff'd*. mem. 614 F.2d 1286 (2d Cir. 1979).

²⁰*Computer Sciences Corporation* v. *Commissioner of Internal Revenue*, 63 T.C. 327 (1974).

²¹Financial Accounting Standards Board, *Statement of Financial Accounting Standards No. 2*, "Accounting for Research and Development Costs" (Stamford, Conn., 1974).

²²Financial Accounting Standards Board, *FASB Interpretation No. 6*, "Applicability of FASB Statement No. 2 to Computer Software" (Stamford, Conn., 1975).

²³Financial Accounting Standards Board, *Technical Bulletin 79-2*, "Computer Software Costs," (Stamford, Conn., 1979).

²⁴At least two federal agencies permit the capitalization of software under certain circumstances. See United States General Accounting Office, *Illustrative Accounting Procedures for Federal Agencies: Guidelines for Automatic Data Processing Costs*, (Federal Government Accounting Pamphlet No. 4, GAO, 1978); also see, Interstate Commerce Commission, *Accounting Series Circulation No. 194*, September 17, 1982, which is discussed in *Motor Freight Controller*, December 1982, p. 14.

²⁵Accounting Principles Board, *APB Opinion No. 17*, "Intangible Assets," (New York: AICPA, 1970).

²⁶Financial Accounting Standards Board, *Statement of Financial Accounting Standards No. 2*, "Accounting for Research and Development Costs," (Stamford, Conn., 1974).

²⁷*FASB Interpretation No. 6*, par. 7.

²⁸Ibid.

²⁹*FASB Technical Bulletin No. 79-2*, par. 3.

³⁰Final Report (1978), p. 10. Also see the last page of the opinion in *Comptroller of the Treasury* v. *Equitable Trust Company*, 464 A.2d 248 (Md. 1983). See also, the dissenting opinion in *James* v. *Tres Computer Systems, Inc.*, 642 S.W.2d 347 (Mo. 1982).

³¹See Karl K. Heinzman, "Computer Software: Should It Be Treated As Tangible Property for Ad Valorem Tax?," *The Journal of Taxation*, September 1972, pp. 184–86; *Commerce Union Bank* v. *Tidwell*, 538 S.W.2d 405 (Tenn. 1976); *District of Columbia* v. *Universal Computer Associates, Inc.*, 465 F.2d 615 (D.C. Cir. 1972); *James* v. *Tres Computer Systems, Inc.*, 642 S.W.2d 347 (Mo. 1982).

³²Financial Accounting Standards Board, *FASB Statement No. 50*, "Financial Reporting in the Record and Music Industry." (Stamford, Conn., 1981), par. 11. Also see, American Institute of Certified Public Accountants, *Statement of Position 76-1*, "Accounting Practices in the Record and Music Industry," (New York: AICPA, 1976).

³³*FASB Statement No. 50*, appendix.

³⁴Coopers & Lybrand, letter to Director of Research and Technical Activities, Financial Accounting Standards Board, dated September 11, 1981.

³⁵See New York State Society of Certified Public Accountants, letter to Director of Research and Technical Activities, Financial Accounting Standards Board, dated August 27, 1981 (File Ref: #1063-077); American Institute of Certified Public Accountants, letter to Michael O. Alexander, Director of Research and Technical Activities, Financial Accounting Standards Board, dated October 15, 1981 (File Ref: #1063-077).

³⁶Arthur Andersen & Company, letter to Director of Research and Technical Activities, Financial Accounting Standards Board, dated September 21, 1981; Arthur Young & Company, letter to Michael O. Alexander, Director of Research and Technical Activities, Financial Accounting Standards Board, dated September 21, 1981.

³⁷*FASB Statement No. 53* (Stamford, Conn., 1981). Also see the following, both by the AICPA: *Industry Accounting Guide*, "Accounting for Motion Picture Films" (1973) and *Statement of Position 79-4*, "Accounting for Motion Picture Films" (1979).

³⁸Ibid., par. 10 and 11.

³⁹Ibid., par. 10 and 13.

⁴⁰Ibid., par. 12.

⁴¹In its comment letter to the Exposure Draft of *Statement No. 53* (dated August 27, 1981—File Ref: #1063-074), the New York State Society of Certified Public Accountants recommended that reference to the periodic-table-computation be deleted, because the film industry generally follows the individual-film-forecast method on a film-by-film basis. The letter also points out that other methods can always be used as long as the result would not be materially different, and any reference to other methods would only add confusion. Arthur Young & Company made a similar comment (letter dated September 21, 1981), as did the Accounting Standards Division of the AICPA (letter dated November 13, 1981). Several respondents to the Exposure Draft also mentioned that reference should be made to interest capitalization costs, *FASB Statement No. 34*.

Even though the periodic-table-computation method might not be the most widely used method in the film industry, it might find acceptance in the software industry, because a larger variety of product is produced in the latter industry.

⁴²See *Bing Crosby Productions, Inc. v. United States*, 79-1 U.S.T.C. 9150, 588 F.2d 1293 (9th Cir. 1979); *Walt Disney Productions v. United States* (Disney I), 327 F. Supp. 189 (C.D. Cal. 1971), *aff'd. as modified*, 480 F.2d 66 (9th Cir. 1973), 32 AFTR2d 73-5094, *cert. denied*, 415 U.S. 934, 94 S. Ct. 1451, 39 L.Ed.2d 493 (1974); *Walt Disney Productions v. United States* (Disney III), 549 F.2d 576 (9th Cir. 1977), 39 AFTR2d 77-796; *Boswell v. Paramount Television Sales, Inc.*, 291 Ala. 490, 282 So.2d 892 (1973); *Florida Association of Broadcasters v. Kirk*, Fla. App. 264 So.2d 437, *cert. denied*, Fla. 268 So.2d 534 (1972); *Crescent Amusement Co. v. Carson*, 187 Tenn. 112, 213 S.W.2d 27 (1948); *In re Merrill Theatre Corp. Sales and Use Tax*, 138 Vt. 397, 415 A.2d 1327 (1980); *Mount Mansfield Television, Inc. v. Vermont Commissioner of Taxes*, 133 Vt. 284, 336 A.2d 193 (1975); *Columbia Pictures Industries, Inc. v. Tax Commissioner*, 176 Conn. 604, 410 A.2d 457 (1979); *United Artists Corp. v. Taylor*, 273 N.Y. 334, N.E.2d 254 (1937); *Turner Communications Corp. v. Chilivis*, 239 Ga. 91, 236 S.E.2d 251 (1977); *Commerce Union Bank v. Tidwell*, 538 S.W.2d 405 (Tenn. 1976); and *Michael Todd Co. v. County of Los Angeles*, 57 Cal. 2d 684, 21 Cal. Rptr. 604, 371 P.2d 340 (1962).

⁴³Financial Accounting Standards Board, *FASB Statement No. 68*, "Research and Development Arrangements," (Stamford, Conn., 1982).

⁴⁴See Chapter 3 of this book.

⁴⁵A spokesman for ITT has revealed that $27.9 million in software-development costs were placed on the balance sheet as assets in 1982, compared to earnings of $702.8 million. See

Richard L. Hudson, "SEC May Curb Accounting Rule for Software," *The Wall Street Journal*, April 8, 1983, p. 52.

⁴⁶Neil E. Paulsen, "Software Development Costs Should Be Capitalized," *Management Accounting*, November 1983, pp. 40–42.

⁴⁷John J. Gannon and David Parkinson, "Software Development Costs Should Be Expensed," *Management Accounting*, November 1983, pp. 37–39.

⁴⁸Naomi Adams, "Programming Computer Software Into Financial Statements," *Going Concerns*, Queens College Accounting Honor Society, October 19, 1983, p. 4; Alex. Brown & Sons, "Industry Accounting Concerns," *Computer Services Monthly*, August 1982; Gary W. Burns and D. Scott Peterson, "Accounting for Computer Software," *The Journal of Accountancy*, April 1982, pp. 50–51, 53–54, 56, 58; "Expenses, Shmexpenses," *Forbes*, May 23, 1983, p. 13; Eamonn Fingleton, "Capital Offense," *Forbes*, January 17, 1983, pp. 100–101; Eamonn Fingleton, "U.S. Laws Hit Hi-Tech," *Accountancy Age*, April 21, 1983, p. 21; Earl K. Littrell, "Death of an Asset—The R&D Blood Bath," *Management Accounting*, January 1981, p. 63; Robert W. McGee, "Accounting for Software—A Progress Report," *Management Accounting*, January 1983, pp. 38, 66; Robert W. McGee, "Accounting for Software Costs Study Is Under Way," *Association Leader*, October 1983, pp. 1, 9; Robert W. McGee, "Software Accounting Is New MAP Project," *Association Leader*, January 1983, pp. 1–2; Roger Neal, "Caution for Lotus-Eaters," *Forbes*, September 26, 1983, pp. 52, 54; Charles Pridemore, "Software: Should Development Costs be Expensed or Capitalized?," *Management Accounting*, November 1983, pp. 33–36.

⁴⁹"Task Force of AcSEC Studies Computer Software Accounting," *The Journal of Accountancy*, June 1983, p. 9.

⁵⁰Securities and Exchange Commission, "Accounting for Costs of Internally Developing Computer Software for Sale or Lease to Others," 17 C.F.R. Parts 210 and 239; Release Nos. 33-6476; 34-20061; FR-12, File No. S7-968. August 8, 1983. Published in the Federal Register Vol. 48, No. 157, August 12, 1983, pp. 36566–36571.

⁵¹Eamonn Fingleton, "Capital Offense," *Forbes*, January 17, 1983, pp. 100–101. Also see Eamonn Fingleton, "U.S. Laws Hit Hi-Tech," *Accountancy Age*, April 21, 1983, p. 21; "Expenses, Shmexpenses," *Forbes*, May 23, 1983, p. 13.

⁵²Bertrand Horwitz and Richard Kolodny, "Has the FASB Hurt Small High-Technology Companies?," *Harvard Business Review*, May/June 1980, pp. 44, 48, 52.

⁵³Robert W. McGee, *The Effects of Software Accounting Policies on Bank Lending Decisions and Stock Price*, (New York: National Association of Accountants, 1984); Abdussalam Ali El-Arabi, "The Effects of Accounting Alternatives on Lending Decisions of Commercial Bankers," Ph.D. dissertation, The Louisiana State University and Agricultural and Mechanical College, 1977; Mostafa El-Maksy, "A Theoretical and Empirical Investigation of the Effects of *FASB Statement No. 33* on Lending Decisions," Ph.D. dissertation, City University of New York, 1983; Tribhowan Nath Jain, "A Study of the Effects of Alternative Methods of Accounting for Income Taxes on Term Loan Decisions," Ph.D. dissertation, Michigan State University, 1970.

⁵⁴Association of Data Processing Service Organizations, "Accounting Guidelines for the Computer Services Industry, *Exposure Draft*, April 1982.

Chapter 3

¹For more detailed statistics, see Robert W. McGee, *Accounting For Software Costs*, (New York: National Association of Accountants, 1984).

²This low response rate for the investment tax credit seems strange in light of the fact that the Internal Revenue Service and at least one court case allow the investment tax credit to be

taken in some instances. See Rev. Proc. 69-21, 1969-2 C.B. 303; Rev. Rul. 71-177, 1971-1 C.B. 5; *Texas Instruments* v. *United States*, 407 F. Supp. 1326 (N.D. Tex. 1976), *rev'd*. 551 F.2d 599, 39 AFTR2d 77-1383 (5th Cir. 1977).

Chapter 5

[1] For more detailed statistics, see Robert W. McGee, *Accounting For Software Costs* (New York: National Association of Accountants, 1984).

[2] See Rev. Proc. 69-21, 1969-2 C.B. 303, T.I.R. No. 1021, October 7, 1969 and Rev. Rul. 71-177, 1971-1 C.B. 5.

[3] *Texas Instruments, Inc.* v. *United States*, 407 F. Supp. 1326, 551 F.2d 599, 39 AFTR2d 77-1383 (5th Cir. 1977).

Chapter 6

[1] J. L. O'Donnell, "Relationships Between Reported Earnings and Stock Prices in the Electric Utility Industry," *The Accounting Review*, January 1965, pp. 135-143.

[2] J. L. O'Donnell, "Further Observation on Reported Earnings and Stock Prices," *The Accounting Review*, July 1968, pp. 549-53.

[3] Edward L. Summers, "Observation of Effects of Using Alternative Reporting Practices," *The Accounting Review*, April 1968, pp. 257-65.

[4] George J. Staubus, "The Association of Financial Accounting Variables with Common Stock Values," *The Accounting Review*, January 1965, pp. 119-34.

[5] R. E. Jensen, "An Experimental Design for Study of Effects of Accounting Variations in Decision Making," *Journal of Accounting Research*, Autumn 1966, pp. 224-38.

[6] W. J. Bruns, Jr., "Inventory Valuation and Management Decisions," *The Accounting Review*, April 1965, pp. 345-57.

[7] T. R. Dyckman, "On the Investment Decisions," *The Accounting Review*, April 1964, pp. 285-95.

[8] T. R. Dyckman, "The Effects of Alternative Accounting Techniques on Certain Management Decisions," *Journal of Accounting Research*, Spring 1964, pp. 91-107.

[9] T. R. Dyckman, "On the Effects of Earnings—Trends, Size and Inventory Valuation Procedures in Evaluating a Business Firm," in *Research in Accounting Measurement* ed. Jaedicke et al. (Sarasota, Fla.: American Accounting Association, 1966), pp. 175-85.

[10] N. Dopuch and J. Ronen, "The Effects of Alternative Inventory Valuation Methods," *Journal of Accounting Research*, Autumn 1973, pp. 191-211.

[11] F. A. Mlynorczyk, "An Empirical Study of Accounting Methods and Stock Prices," *Empirical Research in Accounting: Selected Studies*, 1969, pp. 63-81.

[12] H. Falk and T. Ophir, "The Influence of Differences in Accounting Policies on Investment Decisions," *Journal of Accounting Research*, Spring 1973, pp. 108-116. Also see H. Falk, "Use of Financial Statements for Investment Decision Making in Israel's Companies." Ph.D. dissertation, Hebrew University, 1971.

[13] For a recent study that addressed both bank lending policies and stock price, see Robert W. McGee, *The Effects of Software Accounting Policies on Bank Lending Decisions and Stock Price*, (New York: National Association of Accountants, 1984).

[14] Tribhowan Nath Jain, "A Study of the Effects of Alternative Methods of Accounting for Income Taxes on Term Loan Decisions," Ph.D. dissertation, Michigan State University, 1970.

[15]Abdussalam Ali El-Arabi, "The Effects of Accounting Alternatives on Lending Decisions of Commerical Bankers," Ph.D. dissertation, the Louisiana State University and Agricultural and Mechanical College, 1977.

[16]Mostafa M. El-Maksy, "A Theoretical and Empirical Investigation of the Effects of *FASB Statement No. 33* on Lending Decisions," Ph.D. dissertation, City University of New York, 1983.

[17]Jain, "A Study of the Effects," p. 271. Jain also found no difference between groups for compensating balances, minimum working capital, maximum additional debt, maximum dividends, or maximum officers salaries.

[18]Ibid.

[19]The El-Arabi study found that bank size was not a significant factor in the lending decision.

[20]The El-Maksy and El-Arabi studies found that experience is not a significant factor in the loan decision-making process.

[21]The El-Arabi study found that rank was a significant factor in the lending decision. However, El-Maksy found that sex and membership in a banking association were not significant factors.

[22]The El-Arabi and El-Maksy studies both found that the bank's geographic location is not a significant factor in the lending decision. El-Maksy also found that the amount of time spent responding to the questionnaire was not significant.

[23]For additional studies on the views of bank lenders and financial analysts, see Robert W. McGee, *The Effects of Software Accounting Policies on Bank Lending Decisions and Stock Price* (New York: National Association of Accountants, 1984).

Chapter 7

[1]See Schmedel, "IBM Discloses Plan for Separating Its Computer and Services Prices," *The Wall Street Journal*, June 24, 1969, p. 38; Goetz, "When IBM Unbundled," *Computerworld*, December 31, 1979/January 7, 1980, p. 35; Goetz, "Unbundling: Will 80's Repeat the 60's?," *Computerworld*, April 14, 1980, p. 33.

[2]John G. Martin, "The Revolt Against the Property Tax on Software: An Unnecessary Conflict Growing Out of Unbundling," *Suffolk University Law Review* 9 (Fall 1974), 124.

[3]"Software and Sales Taxes: The Illusory Intangible," *B.U.L. Rev.* 63 (1983), p. 181; Matthew A. Case, "Sales and Use Tax of Computer Software—Is Software Tangible Personal Property," *Wayne Law Review* 27 (Summer 1981), pp. 1503-36; Robert D. Crockett, "Software Taxation: A Critical Reevaluation of the Notion of Intangibility," *Brigham Young University Law Review*, 1980, pp. 859-79; John W. Bryant and Lance R. Mather, "Property Taxation of Computer Software," *New York Law Forum* 18 (Summer 1972), pp. 59-75, reprinted in *The Monthly Digest of Tax Articles*, March 1973, pp. 31-40; "Computer Programs as Goods Under the U.C.C.," *Michigan Law Review* 77 (April 1979) pp. 1149-1165; Arthur R. Rosen, "Computer Software Classed as Intangible Property is Exempt from State Property Taxes," *The Journal of Taxation*, February 1983, pp. 114-16; Michael Vanecek and Debra White, "Software and Taxation: Beware," *Journal of Systems Management*, February 1982, pp. 6-10; Karl K. Heinzman, "Computer Software: Should It Be Taxed As Tangible Personal Property?," *Assessors Journal*, October 1971, pp. 59-64; Karl K. Heinzman, "Computer Software: Should It Be Treated As Tangible Property For Ad Valorem Tax?," *The Journal of Taxation*, September 1972, pp. 184-86.

[4]See Ronald J. Palenski, *Sales and Use Tax Status of Computer Programs by State*, (Arlington, Va.: ADAPSO, 1983). Prewritten programs, also called canned or off-the-shelf pro-

grams, are standardized programs that are sold to many buyers "as is," without alteration. Examples include game cartridges as well as many payroll and accounts receivable programs. Custom programs are individually tailored to meet the needs of an individual customer.

[5] See Daniel A. Beucke, "Custom Software Firms Exempted From State Sales Tax," *San Jose Mercury*, September 23, 1982; Rory J. O'Connor, "California Bill Seeks to End 'Software Tax'," *Computer Business News*, September 13, 1982; Michael Vanecek and Debra White, "Software and Taxation: Beware," *Journal of Systems Management*, February 1982, pp. 6-10; Debra M. White and Michael T. Vanecek, "Taxpayer Beware! The Current State of Computer Software Taxation," *Taxes*, May 1982, pp. 373-77; Edith D. Myers, "Data Processing and Taxes," *Datamation*, May 1977, pp. 155-160; Steven A. Vajda, "Software Sales Tax Issue May Ignite DP," *Data Management*, February 1979, pp. 40-41; Robert Sherin, "Current Status of Software Tax Issue," *Data Management*, January 1978, pp. 110-113; Robert Sherin, "Software Taxes: Let's Tip the Scale Back to Common Sense," *Data Management*, September 1977, pp. 34-36; Herbert B. Safford, "Perspective/Software Taxation," *Data Management*, March 1973, pp. 36, 33; L. Valigra, "Software Tax To Be Tested in California Courts," *Mini-Micro Systems*, September 18, 1981, pp. 36, 43; Edith D. Myers, "Taxes: Spotlight on California," *Datamation*, January 1978, pp. 201-203; Edith D. Myers, " 'We'll Pack the Room,' Says STAG," *Datamation*, February 1978, pp. 183-84; J. Crawford Turner, Jr., "Taxes and Software," *Data Management*, October 1980, p. 58; Franklin L. Green, "Infosystems, the Law and Taxes. . .What's Fair," *Infosystems*, February 1973, pp. 30, 72; Larry A. Welke, "Infosystems, the Law and Taxes. . .Fair Avoidance," *Infosystems*, February 1973, pp. 31, 62, 76; Robert M. Sherin, "Are Software Taxes Inevitable?," *Datamation*, September 1978, Reader Opinion Forum; "Should Software Be Taxed?," *ICP Insiders' Letter*, February 1982, p.1; Don Leavitt, "To Tax or Not to Tax: The Software Question," *Computerworld*, January 28, 1980, pp. SR15, SR22; Nancy French, "Florida Kills Tax on Software, Rules DP Programs 'Intangible'," *Computerworld*, January 17, 1977, pp. 1-2; Nancy French, "Vermont Excludes DP Services From Sales Tax," *Computerworld*, September 5, 1977, p. 11; Robert M. Sherin, "Tennessee Law Taxing Software Violates the Division of Powers," *Computerworld*, May 9, 1977, p. 19; Roy N. Freed, "It's Not Too Late To Salvage Software Tax Situation," *Computerworld*, May 9, 1977, p. 18; Roy N. Freed, "A Legal Perspective on Sales Taxation of Software Programs," *Taxes*, September 1982, pp. 696-99.

[6] "Goods" is defined in U.C.C. Section 2-105.

[7] See "Software Industry Analysis" in *Computer Yearbook* (Saint Clair Shores, Mich.: Scholarly Press, 1972), p. 98.

[8] See C. Sippl and C. Sippl, *Computer Dictionary and Handbook* (Indianapolis, Ind.: Howard W. Sons, 1972), p. 202.

[9] Ibid., p. 407.

[10] Werner L. Frank, *The New Software Economics* 7 (1979).

[11] Rev. Proc. 69-21, 1969-2 C.B. 303.

[12] *American National Dictionary for Information Processing*, American Standards Committee, X3, Technical Report 1-77.

[13] Federal Information Processing Standards Publication 11-1, September 30, 1977.

[14] *Commerce Union Bank* v. *Tidwell*, 538 S.W.2d 405, 406 (Tenn. 1976); See also, *Greyhound Computer Corp.* v. *State Department of Assessments and Taxation*, 271 Md. 674, 320 A.2d 52 (1974).

[15] John W. Bryant and Lance R. Mather, "Property Taxation of Computer Software," *New York Law Forum* 18, (1972) pp. 59, 62.

[16] *Commerce Union Bank* v. *Tidwell*, 538 S.W.2d 405, 406 (Tenn. 1976).

[17] See California Revenue and Tax Code Sections 995, 995.1, 995.2 (West Supp. 1980). This provision taxes systems programs only.

[18] Anthony G. Ferraro, "Software: A Practical Appraisal Viewpoint," *Assessors Journal*, October 1971, p. 65.

[19] Karl K. Heinzman, "Computer Software: Should It Be Taxed As Tangible Personal Property?," *Assessors Journal*, October 1971, p. 59.

[20] N.J. Ad. Code R. 18: 24-25.1, 2 (1980); Cal. Ad. Code R. 1502(F) (1981).

[21] *FASB Interpretation No. 6*: "Applicability of *FASB Statement No. 2* to Computer Software: An Interpretation of *FASB Statement No. 2*, (Stamford, Conn.: 1975).

[22] *FASB Technical Bulletin No. 79-2*: "Computer Software Costs," (Stamford, Conn.: 1979).

[23] Opler has defined firmware as "microprograms resident in the computer's control memory." ("Fourth-Generation Software," *Datamation*, January 1967, p. 22.) Others classify firmware as a portion of systems hardware [J. Adams and D. Haden, *Computers: Appreciation, Applications, Implications*, (1973) p. 260.]

[24] 465 F.2d 615 (D.C. Cir. 1972).

[25] *Commerce Union Bank* v. *Tidwell*, 538 S.W.2d 405 (Tenn. 1976).

[26] 538 S.W.2d 405 at 408.

[27] *First National Bank of Fort Worth* v. *Bullock*, 584 S.W.2d 548 (Tex. Civ. App. 1979).

[28] *District of Columbia* v. *Universal Computer Associates*, 465 F.2d 615 (D.C. Cir. 1972) and *Commerce Union Bank* v. *Tidwell*, 538 S.W.2d 405 (Tenn. 1976) both employed this rationale.

[29] See *District of Columbia* v. *Universal Computer Associates*, 465 F.2d 615 (D.C. Cir. 1972); *Commerce Union Bank* v. *Tidwell*, 538 S.W.2d 405 (Tenn. 1976); *First National Bank of Forth Worth* v. *Bullock*, 584 S.W.2d 548 (Tex. Civ. App. 1979); and *State of Alabama* v. *Central Computer Services, Inc.*, 349 So.2d 1160 (Ala. 1977).

[30] In the course of the interviews conducted in connection with this research project, it was discovered that some corporations use this mode of transmission in order to avoid paying the sales tax.

[31] Whether an otherwise taxable event becomes nontaxable by use of this mode of transmission depends on state law. Some states would treat such transactions as legal tax avoidance, whereas other states might regard it as illegal tax evasion if the tax is not paid on the transfer.

[32] See *Chittenden Trust Company* v. *King*, 465 A.2d 1100 (Vt. 1983); *Commerce Union Bank* v. *Tidwell*, 538 S.W.2d 405 (Tenn. 1976); *Comptroller of the Treasury* v. *Equitable Trust Company*, 464 A.2d 248 (Md. 1983); *First National Bank of Springfield* v. *Department of Revenue*, 85 Ill.2d 84, 421 N.E.2d 175 (1981); *Greyhound Computer Corporation* v. *State Department of Assessments and Taxation*, 320 A.2d 52 (Md. App. 1974), 271 Md. 674 (1974); *James* v. *TRES Computer Service, Inc.*, 642 S.W.2d 347 (Mo. 1982); *State of Alabama* v. *Central Computer Services, Inc.*, 349 So.2d 1160 (1977).

For cases involving the tangibility of films and records for sales, use and property tax purposes, see *Recording Devices* v. *Bowers*, 174 Ohio St. 518, 190 N.E.2d 258 (1963); *Recording Devices* v. *Porterfield*, 30 Ohio St.2d 208, 283 N.E.2d 626 (1972); *Michael Todd Co.* v. *County of Los Angeles*, 57 Cal.2d 684, 21 Cal. Rptr. 604, 371 P.2d 340 (1962); *University Microfilms* v. *Scio Township*, 76 Mich. App. 616, 257 N.W.2d 265 (1977), leave to appeal denied, 402 Mich. 880 (1978); *Boswell* v. *Paramount Television Sales, Inc.*, 291 Ala. 490, 282 So.2d 892 (1973); *Crescent Amusement Co.* v. *Carson*, 187 Tenn. 112, 213 S.W.2d 27 (1948); *United Artists Corp.* v. *Taylor*, 273 N.Y. 334, 7 N.E.2d 254 (1937); *Saenger Realty Corp.* v. *Grosjean*, 194 La. 470, 193 So. 710; *Burgess Co.* v. *Ames*, 359 Ill. 427, 194 N.E. 565; *District of Columbia* v. *Norwood Studios, Inc.*, 336 F.2d 746 (D.C. Cir. 1964); *Simplicity Pattern Company, Inc.* v. *State Board of Equalization*, 101 Cal. App.3d 184, 161 Cal. Rptr. 558 (1980).

For cases involving tangibility for investment tax credit purposes, see *Walt Disney Productions* v. *United States* (Disney I), 327 F. Supp. 189 (C.D. Cal. 1971), aff'd. as modified, 480 F.2d 66 (9th Cir. 1973), 32 AFTR2d 73-5094, cert. denied, 415 U.S. 934, 94 S.Ct. 1451, 39

L.Ed. 493 (1974); *Walt Disney Productions* v. *United States* (Disney III), 549 F.2d 576 (9th Cir. 1977), 39 AFTR2d 77-796; *Texas Instruments, Inc.* v. *United States*, 551 F.2d 599, 39 AFTR2d 77-1383 (5th Cir. 1977); *Bing Crosby Productions, Inc.* v. *United States*, 588 F.2d 1293 (9th Cir. 1979), 79-1 USTC 9150; *Sussex Pictures, Inc.* v. *United States*, 588 F.2d 1293 (9th Cir. 1979), 79-1 USTC 9150; and *MCA, Inc. and Universal City Studios, Inc.* v. *United States*, 588 F.2d 1293 (9th Cir. 1979), 79-1 USTC 9150.

For a case involving tangibility of computer software for collapsible corporation purposes, see *Computer Sciences Corporation* v. *Commissioner of Internal Revenue*, 63 T.C. 327 (1974).

For an analogy of films and records to software for financial and managerial accounting purposes, see Robert W. McGee, *Accounting for Software Costs*, (New York: National Association of Accountants, 1984).

[33] Films, records, and books are generally treated as tangible property for sales tax purposes.

[34] See Karl K. Heinzman, "Computer Software: Should It Be Treated As Tangible Property For Ad Valorem Tax?" *The Journal of Taxation*, September 1972, p. 185; John W. Bryant and Lance R. Mather, "Property Taxation of Computer Software." *New York Law Forum* 18 (Summer 1972), p. 74; *Commerce Union Bank* v. *Tidwell*, 538 S.W.2d 405 (Tenn. 1976), at p. 407–408; Statement of the Business Equipment Manufacturers Association (BEMA) to the State of California—State Board of Equalization *In re*: Proposed Rule 32 (January 18, 1972); John W. Bryant and Lance R. Mather, "Property Taxation of Computer Software," *The Monthly Digest of Tax Articles*, March 1973, pp. 31–40; Karl K. Heinzman, "Computer Software: Should It Be Taxed As Tangible Personal Property?" *Assessors Journal*, October 1971, pp. 59–64; Matthew A. Case, "Sales and Use Tax of Computer Software—Is Software Tangible Personal Property?" *Wayne Law Review* 27 (Summer 1981), p. 1516.

[35] See *District of Columbia* v. *Universal Computer Associates, Inc.*, 465 F.2d 615 (D.C. Cir. 1972) and *Commerce Union Bank* v. *Tidwell*, 538 S.W.2d 405 (Tenn. 1976).

[36] 538 S.W.2d 405 at 408. This analogy assumes that the program, once run, is stored in the computer's memory.

[37] See *Alabama* v. *Central Computer Services, Inc.*, 349 So.2d 1160 at 1162 (Ala. 1977); *Commerce Union Bank* v. *Tidwell*, 538 S.W.2d 405 at 408 (Tenn. 1976). In *University Microfilms* v. *Scio Township*, 76 Mich. App. 616, 257 N.W.2d 265 (1977), *leave to appeal denied*, 402 Mich. 880 (1978), the court distinguished software from master microfilm negatives, noting that "[t]he value of plaintiff's master negatives is in the printed word itself."

[38] See Matthew A. Case, "Sales and Use Tax of Computer Software—Is Software Tangible Personal Property?" *Wayne Law Review* 27 (Summer 1981), p. 1518.

[39] John W. Bryant and Lance R. Mather, "Property Taxation of Computer Software," *New York Law Forum* 18 (Summer 1972), p. 74. An abbreviated version of this article was reprinted in *The Monthly Digest of Tax Articles*, March 1973, pp. 31–40.

[40] See *Accountants Computer Services, Inc.* v. *Kosydar, Central Data Systems, Inc.* v. *Kosydar*, and *The Andrew Jergens Co.* v. *Kosydar*, all reported at 35 Ohio St.2d 120, 298 N.E.2d 519 (1973); *Bullock* v. *Statistical Tabulating Corp.*, 549 S.W.2d 166 (Texas 1977); *Janesville Data Center, Inc.* v. *Wisconsin Department of Revenue*, 84 Wis.2d 341, 267 N.W.2d 656 (1978); *Nova Computing Services, Inc.* v. *Askew*, Florida Division of Administrative Hearings, No. 76-1475 (1976); *Citizens Financial Corp.* v. *Kosydar*, 43 Ohio St.2d 148, 331 N.E.2d 435 (1975); *Credit Bureau of Miami County, Inc.* v. *Collins*, 50 Ohio St.2d 270, 364 N.E.2d 27 (1977); *Intellidata, Inc.* v. *State Board of Equalization*, 139 Cal. App.3d 594, 188 Cal. Rptr. 850 (1983); *Miami Citizens National Bank* v. *Lindley*, 50 Ohio St.2d 249, 364 N.E.2d 25 (1977).

[41] The Uniform Commercial Code (UCC) distinguishes the sale of goods from the sale of services. For UCC cases that have been cited in cases addressing the issue of software taxation, see *Helvey* v. *Wabash County REMC*, 151 Ind. App. 176, 278 N.E.2d 608 (1972); *Carl Beasley*

Ford, Inc. v. *Burroughs Corporation*, 361 F.Supp. 325 (E.D. Pa. 1973), *aff'd.* 493 F.2d 1400 (3d Cir. 1974); *F & M Schaefer Corp.* v. *Electronic Data Systems Corp.*, 430 F.Supp. 988 (S.D. N.Y. 1977), *aff'd.* mem. 614 F.2d 1286 (2d Cir. 1979); *Triangle Underwriters, Inc.* v. *Honeywell, Inc.*, 457 F.Supp. 765 (E.D. N.Y. 1978), *rev'd. on other grounds*, 604 F.2d 737 (2d Cir. 1979).

[42]For cases involving the sale of mailing lists, see *Fingerhut Products Company* v. *Commissioner of Revenue*, 258 N.W.2d 606 (Minn. 1977); *Spencer Gifts, Inc.* v. *Director, Division of Taxation*, 182 N.J. Super. 179, 440 A.2d 104 (N.J. Tax Ct. 1981); *Mertz* v. *State Tax Commission*, 89 A.D.2d 396, 456 N.Y.S.2d 501 (1982). For cases involving the sale of stock exchange information, see *Dun & Bradstreet* v. *City of New York*, 276 N.Y. 198, 11 N.E.2d 728 (1937); *Bunker-Ramo Corp.* v. *Porterfield*, 21 Ohio St.2d 231, 257 N.E.2d 365 (1970); *Quotron Systems* v. *Comptroller*, 287 Md. 178, 411 A.2d 439 (1980). Other cases addressing the product versus service issue are *Washington Times-Herald* v. *District of Columbia*, 94 U.S. App. D.C. 154, 213 F.2d 23 (1954) (artwork); *Southern Bell Telephone and Telegraph Company* v. *Department of Revenue*, 366 So.2d 30 (Fla. Dist. Ct. App. 1978) (artwork); *General Data Corp.* v. *Porterfield*, 21 Ohio St.2d 233, 257 N.E.2d 359 (1970) (hotel reservation information); *Credit Bureau of Miami County, Inc.* v. *Collins*, 50 Ohio St.2d 270, 364 N.E.2d 27 (1977) (credit information).

[43]*Howitt* v. *Street & Smith Publications, Inc.*, 276 N.Y. 345, 12 N.E.2d 435 (1938); *Bigsby* v. *Johnson*, 99 P.2d 268 (1940), *rev'd. on a different issue*, 18 Cal.2d 860, 118 P.2d 289 (1941). See also Matthew A. Case, "Sales and Use Tax of Computer Software—Is Software Tangible Personal Property?," *Wayne Law Review* 27 (Summer 1981), p. 1520.

[44]*Berry-Kofron Dental Lab. Co.* v. *Smith*, 345 Mo. 922, 137 S.W.2d 452, (1940); *Mahon* v. *Nudelman*, 377 Ill. 331, 36 N.E.2d 550 (1941); *Community Telecasting Service* v. *Johnson*, 220 A.2d 500 (Me. 1966); *District of Columbia* v. *Universal Computer Associates, Inc.*, 465 F.2d 615 (D.C. Cir. 1972); *Commerce Union Bank* v. *Tidwell*, 538 S.W.2d 405 (Tenn. 1976).

[45]*United Aircraft Corp.* v. *O'Connor*, 141 Conn. 530, 107 A.2d 398 (1954); *Bucyrus-Erie Co.* v. *Lorenz*, 26 Ill.2d 183, 186 N.E.2d 250 (1962); *University Microfilms* v. *Scio Township*, 76 Mich. App. 616, 257 N.W.2d 265 (1977), *leave to appeal denied*, 402 Mich. 880 (1978).

[46]273 N.Y. 334, 7 N.E.2d 254 (1937).

[47]194 La. 470, 193 So. 710 (1940), *appeal dismissed*, 310 U.S. 613, 60 S.Ct. 1089 (1940). Also see *Bigsby* v. *Johnson*, 99 P.2d 268 (1940), *rev'd. on a different issue*, 18 Cal.2d 860, 118 P.2d 289 (1941); *People ex. rel. Walker Engraving Corp.* v. *Graves*, 243 App. Div. 652, 276 N.Y.S. 674, 268 N.Y. 648, 198 N.E. 539 (1939); *Voss* v. *Gray*, 70 N.D. 727, 298 N.W. 1 (1941); *Cusick* v. *Commonwealth*, 260 Ky. 204, 84 S.W.2d 14 (1935); *State Tax Commission* v. *Hopkins*, 234 Ala. 556, 176 So. 210.

[48]187 Tenn. 112, 213 S.W.2d 27 (1948). The appellant (Crescent) argued unsuccessfully that the rental of a film is a license rather than the transfer of tangible personal property. In *Burgess Co.* v. *Ames*, 359 Ill. 427, 194 N.E. 565 (1935), a case cited by appellant, it was held that the right to reproduce a musical composition is a license rather than a transfer of tangible personal property. Also cited were *A.B.C. Electrotype Co.* v. *Ames*, 364 Ill. 360, 4 N.E.2d 476 (1936) and *Adair* v. *Ames*, 364 Ill. 342, 4 N.E.2d 481 (1936), which held that printers and electrotypers, respectively, are engaged in furnishing skill and labor rather than tangible personalty in the printed matter produced.

[49]213 S.W.2d 27 at 29. Also see *Saverio* v. *Carson*, 186 Tenn. 166, 208 S.W.2d 1018 (1948). In 1951, the legislature changed the result in *Crescent* by exempting theaters which pay the 2 percent privilege tax from operation of the sales and use tax. T.C.A. Sec. 67-3013. However, the present Tennessee Code [Sec. 67-3002(b)] taxes both prewritten and custom programs.

[50]57 Cal.2d 684, 21 Cal. Rptr. 604, 371 P.2d 340 (1962).

⁵¹*Roehm* v. *County of Orange*, 32 Cal.2d 280, 196 P.2d 550 (1948). In this case, the court stated that: "Intangible values . . . that cannot be separately taxed as property may be reflected in the valuation of taxable property. Thus, in determining the value of property, assessing authorities may take into consideration earnings derived therefrom, which may depend upon the possession of intangible rights and privileges that are not themselves regarded as a separate class of taxable property."

⁵²336 F.2d 746 (D.C. Cir. 1964).

⁵³In a prior case decided by this same Circuit Court of Appeals [*Washington Times-Herald* v. *District of Columbia*, 94 U.S. App. D.C. 154, 213 F.2d 23 (1954)], a different conclusion was reached where "mats" were furnished (but not sold) to newspapers for printing comic strips on a one-time basis. The court reasoned that the sale of all interests constitutes a sale for sales tax purposes, but the sale of a one-time right to use property does not.

⁵⁴See *Boswell* v. *Paramount Television Sales, Inc.*, 291 Ala. 490, 282 So.2d 892 (1973). In its opinion, the Alabama court cited *United Artists Corp.* v. *Taylor*, 273 N.Y. 334, 7 N.E.2d 254 (1937), and *Crescent Amusement Co.* v. *Carson*, 187 Tenn. 112, 213 S.W.2d 27 (1948).

⁵⁵490 S.W.2d 796 (1973).

⁵⁶Ibid. at 799.

⁵⁷*University Microfilms* v. *Scio Township*, 76 Mich. App. 616, 257 N.W.2d 265 (1977), *leave to appeal denied*, 402 Mich. 880 (1978).

⁵⁸*Bay Trust Co.* v. *Bay City*, 280 Mich. 44, 273 N.W. 437 (1937); *Loomis* v. *City of Jackson*, 130 Mich. 594, 90 N.W. 328 (1902); *Perry* v. *Big Rapids*, 67 Mich. 146, 34 N.W. 530 (1887); *Dart* v. *Woodhouse*, 40 Mich. 339, 29 Am. Rep. 544 (1879).

⁵⁹*District of Columbia* v. *Universal Computer Associates, Inc.*, 151 U.S. App. D.C. 30, 465 F.2d 615 (1972); *Texas Instruments, Inc.* v. *United States*, 407 F.Supp. 1326 (N.D. Tex. 1976); *Greyhound Computer Corp.* v. *State Department of Assessments and Taxation*, 271 Md. 674, 320 A.2d 52 (1974).

⁶⁰327 F.Supp. 189 (C.D. Cal. 1971), *aff'd. as modified*, 480 F.2d 66 (9th Cir. 1973), 32 AFTR2d 73-5094, *Cert. denied*, 415 U.S. 934, 94 S.Ct. 1451, 39 L.Ed.2d 493 (1974). As a result of this case, Regulation 1.48-1(F), which treats motion picture film negatives as intangible, was declared invalid. A few years later, the Fifth Circuit Court of Appeals agreed with the Disney decision and also held the regulation to be invalid. See *Texas Instruments, Inc.* v. *United States*, 551 F.2d 599, 39 AFTR2d 77-1383 (5th Cir. 1977).

When Congress reenacted the investment tax credit in 1971, it expressly indicated its agreement with the Disney holding that motion pictures and TV films are tangible personal property eligible for the investment tax credit. See S.Rep. No. 92-437, 92d Cong., 1st Sess. 34, 1971 U.S. Code Cong. and Adm. News, pp. 1918, 1941 (1971). Furthermore, the Tax Reform Act of 1976 added Section 48(K) to the Internal Revenue Code, which treats motion picture and TV films as tangible personal property eligible for the investment tax credit. See also Treasury Regulation Section 7.48-1(a).

⁶¹549 F.2d 576 (9th Cir. 1977), 39 AFTR2d 77-796. Other Ninth Circuit cases involving similar issues have reached similar conclusions. See *Bing Crosby Productions, Inc.* v. *United States*, and *MCA, Inc. and Universal City Studios, Inc.* v. *United States*, 588 F.2d 1293 (9th Cir. 1979), 79-1 USTC 9150. For a sales tax case involving the tangibility of master negatives, see *Simplicity Pattern Company, Inc.* v. *State Board of Equalization*, 101 Cal. App.3d 184, 161 Cal. Rptr. 558 (1980).

⁶²276 N.Y. 198, 11 N.E.2d 728 (1937).

⁶³276 N.Y. 205, 11 N.E.2d 731 (1937).

⁶⁴See *Commerce Union Bank* v. *Tidwell*, 538 S.W.2d 405 (Tenn. 1976); *Williams and Lee Scouting Service, Inc.* v. *Calvert*, 452 S.W.2d 789 (Tex. Civ. App. 1970).

⁶⁵*Time, Inc.* v. *Hulman*, 31 Ill.2d 344 at 350 (1964).

⁶⁶*Bunker-Ramo Corp.* v. *Porterfield*, 21 Ohio St.2d 231, 257 N.E.2d 365 (1970).

⁶⁷15 Ohio St.2d 92, 238 N.E.2d 782 (1968).

⁶⁸162 Ohio St. 245, 122 N.E.2d 787 (1954).

⁶⁹174 Ohio St. 518, 190 N.E.2d 258 (1963).

⁷⁰257 N.E.2d 368 (1970).

⁷¹287 Md. 178, 411 A.2d 439 (1980).

⁷²241 Md. 345, 216 A.2d 717 (1966).

⁷³See *Askew* v. *Bell*, 248 So.2d 501 (Fla. Dist. Ct. App. 1971); *Spagat* v. *Mahin*, 50 Ill.2d 183, 277 N.E.2d 834 (1971); *J. H. Walters & Co.* v. *Department of Revenue*, 44 Ill.2d 95, 254 N.E.2d 485 (1969); *Dun & Bradstreet* v. *City of New York*, 276 N.Y. 198, 11 N.E.2d 728 (1937). See also *Undercofler* v. *Grantham Transfer Co.*, 114 Ga. App. 868, 152 S.E.2d 900 (1966); *Machinery Moving, Inc.* v. *Porterfield*, 26 Ohio St.2d 99, 269 N.E.2d 418 (1971).

⁷⁴*J. H. Walters & Co.* v. *Department of Revenue*, 44 Ill.2d 95 at 104-105, 254 N.E.2d 485 at 491 (1969); *Community Telecasting Service* v. *Johnson*, 220 A.2d 500 at 503 (1966); *Dun & Bradstreet* v. *City of New York*, 276 N.Y. 198 at 205, 11 N.E.2d 728 at 731 (1937).

⁷⁵398 Ill. 41, 46, 74 N.E.2d 877, 879-880 (1947). See *General Data Corp* v. *Porterfield*, 21 Ohio St.2d 233, 257 N.E.2d 359 (1970), which involved the installation and use of computer equipment used almost exclusively for the dissemination of hotel reservation information.

⁷⁶50 Ohio St.2d 270, 364 N.E.2d 27 (1977).

⁷⁷The holding in this case is based on the reasoning set forth in *Accountants Computer Services, Inc.* v. *Kosydar*, 35 Ohio St.2d 120, 298 N.E.2d 519 (1973), discussed below.

⁷⁸258 N.W.2d 606 (Minn. 1977).

⁷⁹276 N.Y. 198, 11 N.E.2d 728 (1937).

⁸⁰258 N.W.2d 610.

⁸¹182 N.J. Super. 179, 440 A.2d 104 (N.J. Tax Ct. 1981). Also see *Alan Drey Co., Inc.* v. *State Tax Commission*, 67 A.D.2d 1055, 413 N.Y.S.2d 516, 47 N.Y.2d 708, 418 N.Y.S.2d 1024, 392 N.E.2d 887 (N.Y. App. Div. 1979). A subsequent New York decision [*Mertz* v. *State Tax Commission*, 89 A.D.2d 396, 456 N.Y.S.2d 501 (A.D. 1982)] concluded that its decision in *Alan Drey* should be construed as holding that the transactions involving computer tapes constituted sales of information, while those involving gummed labels constituted sales of tangible personal property. In New York, the sale of information is a taxable event.

⁸²*Mertz* v. *State Tax Commission*, 89 A.D.2d 396, 456 N.Y.S.2d 501 (A.D. 1982).

⁸³Tax Law, Sec. 1105, subd. (c), par. (1).

⁸⁴See *Commerce Union Bank* v. *Tidwell*, 538 S.W.2d 405 (Tenn. 1976); *District of Columbia* v. *Universal Computer Associates*, 465 F.2d 615 (D.C. Cir. 1972).

⁸⁵94 U.S. App. D.C. 154, 213 F.2d 23 (1954).

⁸⁶94 U.S. App. D.C. 155, 213 F.2d 24 (1954).

⁸⁷366 So.2d 30 (Fla. Dist. Ct. App. 1978).

⁸⁸The court determined that Southern Bell met all three tests. In support of its position, the court cited *Askew* v. *Bell*, 248 So.2d 501 (Fla. 1st DCA 1971), where the court held that a court reporter, who for a fee, records a judicial or administrative proceeding, or takes down and transcribes testimony, is engaged in rendering a service, and the transcript which he furnishes to the persons who employ him is a mere incident of that service. The *Askew* court held that such a transaction would be subject to sales tax only when transcripts are sold to third persons who are not parties to the proceeding for which the court reporter was engaged.

The court also cited *Nova Computing Services* v. *Askew, D.O.A.*, Case No. 76-1475: March 1, 1977, which is discussed later.

⁸⁹Section 2-105(1). For a detailed analysis of this aspect of software, see "Computer Programs as Goods Under the U.C.C.," *Michigan Law Review* 77 (April 1979), pp. 1149-65.

⁹⁰151 Ind. App. 176, 278 N.E.2d 608 (1972). Also see *Wivagg* v. *Duquesne Light Co.*, 73 Pa. D. & C.2d 694 (1975); *Buckeye Union Fire Insurance Co.* v. *Detroit Edison Co.*, 38 Mich. App. 325, 196 N.W.2d 316 (1972). The court in *Gardiner* v. *Philadelphia Gas Works*, 413 Pa. 415, 197 A.2d 612 (1964) made the analogy of electricity in wires to natural gas in pipes. Natural gas has been held to be a good.

⁹¹See *Commerce Union Bank* v. *Tidwell*, 538 S.W.2d 405 (Tenn. 1976); *Comptroller of the Treasury* v. *Equitable Trust Company, 464 A.2d 248 (Md. 1983); Chittenden Trust Company* v. *King*, 465 A.2d 1100 (Vt. 1983); *District of Columbia* v. *Universal Computer Associates*, 465 F.2d 615 (D.C. Cir. 1972); Robert D. Crockett, "Software Taxation: A Critical Reevaluation of the Notion of Intangibility," *Brigham Young University Law Review* no. 4, (1980), pp. 859-879; Karl K. Heinzman, "Computer Software: Should It Be Treated As Tangible Property For Ad Valorem Tax?," *The Journal of Taxation*, September 1972, pp. 184-86.

⁹²361 F.Supp. 325 (E.D. Pa. 1973), *aff'd.* 493 F.2d 1400 (3d Cir. 1974). Also see *Burroughs Corporation* v. *Joseph Uram Jewelers, Inc.*, 305 So.2d 215 (Fla. Dist. Ct. App. 1974). The Uniform Commercial Code provision relating to breach of contract applies only to the sale of goods, not services.

⁹³430 F.Supp. 988 (S.D.N.Y. 1977), *aff'd. mem.*, 614 F.2d 1286 (2d Cir. 1979). If held to be intangible, the computer system in question could not have been replevied.

⁹⁴*Triangle Underwriters, Inc.* v. *Honeywell, Inc.*, 457 F.Supp. 765 (E.D.N.Y. 1978), *rev'd. on other grounds*, 604 F.2d 737 (2d Cir. 1979).

⁹⁵468 F.2d 695, 697 (2d Cir. 1972).

⁹⁶See *Dynamics Corporation of America* v. *International Harvester Co.*, 429 F.Supp. 341 (S.D.N.Y. 1977).

⁹⁷479 F.Supp. 738 (D.N.J. 1979), 635 F.2d 1081 (1980).

⁹⁸See *Atlas Industries, Inc.* v. *National Cash Register*, 216 Kan. 213, 531 P.2d 41 (1975) and *Acme Pump Company, Inc.* v. *National Cash Register*, 32 Conn. Sup. 69, 337 A.2d 672 (C.C.P. 1974).

⁹⁹*Accountants Computer Services, Inc.* v. *Kosydar; Central Data Systems, Inc.* v. *Kosydar*; and, *The Andrew Jergens Co.* v. *Kosydar*, all cited as 35 Ohio St.2d 120, 298 N.E.2d 519 (1973). The three cases involved similar issues and were tried simultaneously.

¹⁰⁰*Goodyear Aircraft Corp.* v. *Arizona State Tax Commission*, 1 Ariz. App. 302, 306, 402 P.2d 423, 427 (1965).

¹⁰¹*Rice* v. *Evatt* falls in the second of the three categories mentioned above. It involved an optometrist who did not separate his charge for professional examination from his charge for glasses and other items of personal property transferred. Two separate and distinct transactions were being performed therein—one, a purely professional service; and the other, purely a sale of tangible personal property. The fact that the two transactions were not billed separately is of no consequence in determining the taxability of the transactions.

¹⁰²See *Recording Devices* v. *Bowers*, 174 Ohio St. 518, 190 N.E.2d 258 (1963); *Recording Devices* v. *Porterfield*, 30 Ohio St.2d 208, 283 N.E.2d 626 (1972); *Columbus Coated Fabrics* v. *Porterfield*, 30 Ohio St.2d 307, 285 N.E.2d 50 (1972); and *Koch* v. *Kosydar*, 32 Ohio St.2d 74, 290 N.E.2d 847 (1972).

¹⁰³43 Ohio St.2d 148, 331 N.E.2d 435 (1975). For an in depth analysis of this case, see Michael J. Bayer, "Citizens Financial Corporation v. Kosydar: Data Processing and the Ohio Sales Tax Service Exemption," *Capital University Law Review* 6 (1977), pp. 663-72.

¹⁰⁴35 Ohio St.2d 120, 298 N.E.2d 519 (1973).

[105]32 Ohio St.2d 74, 290 N.E.2d 847 (1972). In *Koch*, the court defined a personal service as "an act done personally by an individual . . . involving either the intellectual or manual personal effort of an individual." (32 Ohio St.2d at 78, 290 N.E.2d at 850).

[106]41 Ohio St.2d 68, 322 N.E.2d 668 (1975).

[107]*Nova Computing Services* v. *Askew, D.O.A.*, Case No. 76-1475: March 1, 1977.

[108]549 S.W.2d 166 (Texas 1977). In *Janesville Data Center, Inc.* v. *Wisconsin Department of Revenue*, 84 Wis.2d 341, 267 N.W.2d 656 (1978), an almost identical fact pattern produced the same result as in *Bullock*. In *Janesville*, customers were given a slight discount if they supplied their own cards.

For a contrary result having a similar fact pattern, see *Intellidata Incorporated* v. *State Board of Equalization*, 139 Cal. App.3d 594, 188 Cal. Rptr. 850 (1983). The California view is that the entire transaction may be treated as tangible even though virtually all of the value is attributed to an intangible element such as intellectual content. This view was used in *People* v. *Grazer*, 138 Cal. App.2d 274, 291 P.2d 957 (1956) [radiologist's X-ray films]; *Albers* v. *State Board of Equalization*, 237 Cal. App.2d 4○4, 47 Cal. Rptr. 69 (1965) [draftsman drawings]; *Simplicity Pattern Co.* v. *State Board of Equalization*, 27 Cal.3d 900, 167 Cal. Rptr. 366, 615 P.2d 555 (1980) [master audiovisual negatives].

[109]452 S.W.2d 789 (Tex. Civ. App. 1970). In *Williams and Lee Scouting*, the court found that the object of the transaction for the plaintiff's subscribing customers was the scouting service provided by plaintiff. Current statistical data on oil and gas well production was continuously gathered in the field by Williams and Lee Scouting Service employees. The data was compiled and mailed to subscribing customers in regular reports duplicated by offset printing at the plaintiff's office. The comptroller (Calvert) attempted to tax the whole transaction because a tangible item, the printed report, changed hands.

For a similar case involving credit report information, see *Credit Bureau of Miami County, Inc.* v. *Collins*, 50 Ohio St.2d 270, 364 N.E.2d 27 (1977).

[110]50 Ohio St.2d 249, 364 N.E.2d 25 (1977).

[111]In support of its position, the court cited *Accountants Computer Services* v. *Kosydar*, 35 Ohio St.2d 120, 298 N.E.2d 519 (1973); *Citizens Financial Corp.* v. *Kosydar*, 43 Ohio St.2d 148, 331 N.E.2d 435 (1975); *Federated Department Stores* v. *Kosydar*, 45 Ohio St.2d 1, 340 N.E.2d 840 (1976); and *Lindner Brothers* v. *Kosydar*, 46 Ohio St.2d 162, 346 N.E.2d 690 (1976).

[112]See Schmedel, "IBM Discloses Plan for Separating Its Computer and Services Prices," *The Wall Street Journal*, June 24, 1969, p. 38.

[113]465 F.2d 615 (D.C. Cir. 1972).

[114]94 U.S. App. D.C. 154, 213 F.2d 23 (1954).

[115]118 U.S. App. D.C. 358, 336 F.2d 746 (1964).

[116]32 Cal. App.3d 654, 108 Cal. Rptr. 434 (1973).

[117]*Greyhound Computer Corporation* v. *State Department of Assessments and Taxation*, 271 Md. 674, 320 A.2d 52 (1974).

[118]For analogies to the film-making industry the court cited *Michael Todd Co.* v. *County of Los Angeles*, 57 Cal.2d 684, 21 Cal. Rptr. 604, 371 P.2d 340 (1962) and *District of Columbia* v. *Norwood Studios, Inc.*, 118 U.S. App. D.C. 358, 336 F.2d 746 (1964). This analogy was challenged in Heinzman, "Computer Software: Should It Be Treated As Tangible Property For Ad Valorem Tax?," *Journal of Taxation* 184 (1972) pp. 185-186.

[119]538 S.W.2d 405 (Tenn. 1976).

[120]187 Tenn. 112, 213 S.W.2d 27 (1948).

[121]See *District of Columbia* v. *Universal Computer Associates, Inc.*, 151 U.S. App. D.C. 30, 465 F.2d 615 (1972).

[122]See *Washington Times-Herald, Inc.* v. *District of Columbia*, 94 U.S. App. D.C. 154, 213 F.2d 23 (1954). There, the newspaper had purchased from an artist the right to reproduce his cartoons. These cartoons were transferred to the newspaper and were physically embodied in mats which were then used to reproduce the cartoons in the newspaper. In that case, the court held that what the newspaper had purchased was the right to reproduce the cartoons, and not the material upon which the cartoons were impressed.

In a closely analogous case, *Dun & Bradstreet* v. *City of New York*, 276 N.Y. 198, 11 N.E.2d 728 (1937), the New York Court of Appeals held that financial informational services rendered to clients of Dun & Bradstreet were nontaxable even though reference books containing financial information were delivered to subscribers. No separate charge was made for the books, and they could not be obtained without subscribing to the service. Also, in that case, as here, the same service could have been rendered without transferring the reference books, but the cost of the service would have been much higher.

The result in this case was subsequently changed by Tenn. Code Sec. 67-3002(b), which calls for the sales taxation of both prewritten and custom programs.

[123]349 So.2d 1160 (1977). This case was a case of first impression in Alabama (meaning no case having a similar fact pattern had previously been tried in Alabama). The court's decision was influenced by *Commerce Union Bank* v. *Tidwell*, 538 S.W.2d 405 (Tenn. 1976) and *District of Columbia* v. *Universal Computer Associates, Inc.*, 151 U.S. App. D.C. 30, 465 F.2d 615 (1972). *Commerce Union Bank* v. *Tidwell* held that computer software is intangible and, therefore, not subject to the Tennessee sales tax.

[124]291 Ala. 490, 282 So.2d 892 (1973).

[125]349 So.2d at 1162. Note: Alabama Rule C28-001 presently exempts both prewritten and custom programs from sales and use taxation.

[126]549 S.W.2d 166 (Tex. 1977).

[127]584 S.W.2d 548 (Tex. Civ. App. 1979).

[128]Tex. Tax—Gen. Ann. art. 20.01(P) (1969).

[129]*Bullock* v. *Statistical Tabulating Corp.*, 549 S.W.2d 166 (Tex. 1977).

[130]*Williams and Lee Scouting Service, Inc.* v. *Calvert*, 452 S.W.2d 789 (Tex. Civ. App. 1970).

[131]*State of Alabama* v. *Central Computer Services, Inc.*, 349 So.2d 1160 (Ala. 1977); *Commerce Union Bank* v. *Tidwell*, 538 S.W.2d 405 (Tenn. 1976).

[132]*District of Columbia* v. *Universal Computer Associates, Inc.* 151 U.S. App. D.C. 30, 465 F.2d 615 (1972); *Commerce Union Bank* v. *Tidwell*, 538 S.W.2d 405 (Tenn. 1976).

[133]85 Ill.2d 84, 421 N.E.2d 175 (1981).

[134]In its argument, the Department cited *Time, Inc.* v. *Hulman*, 31 Ill.2d 344 (1964), where the Illinois court decided that magazines are tangible personal property and that the proceeds from their sale would be subject to the retailers' occupation tax were it not for an exclusion afforded to newspapers and other materials "such as" newsprint.

[135]*Ingersoll Milling Machine Co.* v. *Department of Revenue*, 405 Ill. 367 (1950).

[136]See John W. Bryant and Lance R. Mather, "Property Taxation of Computer Software," *New York Law Forum* 18 (Summer 1972), pp. 59–75; reprinted in *The Monthly Digest of Tax Articles*, March 1973, pp. 31–40.

[137]In support of its position, the court cited: *First National Bank* v. *Bullock*, 584 S.W.2d 548 (Tex. Civ. App. 1979); *Janesville Data Center, Inc.* v. *Wisconsin Department of Revenue*, 84 Wis. 341, 287 N.W.2d 656 (1978); *Honeywell Information Systems, Inc.* v. *Maricopa County*, 118 Ariz. 171, 575 P.2d 801 (1978); *State* v. *Central Computer Services, Inc.*, 349 So.2d 1160 (Ala. 1977); *Commerce Union Bank* v. *Tidwell*, 538 S.W.2d 405 (Tenn. 1976); *District of Columbia* v. *Universal Computer Associates, Inc.*, 465 F.2d 615 (D.C. Cir. 1972); *County of*

Sacramento v. *Assessment Appeals Board No. 2*, 32 Cal. App.3d 654, 108 Cal. Rptr. 434 (1973). Also cited was Cal. Revenue & Tax Code Secs. 995, 995.1 and 995.2 (West. Supp. 1974), which subjects operational software to property taxation, but exempts applicational software. See also *Honeywell, Inc. v. Lithonia Lighting, Inc.*, 317 F.Supp. 406 (N.D. Ga. 1970); also, *Greyhound Computer Corp. v. State Department of Assessments and Taxation*, 271 Md. 674, 320 A.2d 52 (1974), which held that only so much of software as consists of services is intangible and not taxable.

[138] 642 S.W.2d 347 (Mo. 1982).

[139] *State of Alabama v. Central Computer Services, Inc.*, 349 So.2d 1160 (Ala. 1977); *Commerce Union Bank v. Tidwell*, 538 S.W.2d 405 (Tenn. 1976); *Bullock v. Statistical Tabulating Corp.*, 549 S.W.2d 166 (Tex. 1977); *First National Bank of Fort Worth v. Bullock*, 584 S.W.2d 548 (Tex. Civ. App. 1979); *First National Bank of Springfield v. Department of Revenue*, 85 Ill.2d 84, 51 Ill. Dec. 667, 421 N.E.2d 175 (1981); *District of Columbia v. Universal Computer Associates, Inc.*, 151 U.S. App. D.C. 30, 465 F.2d 615 (1972); *Janesville Data Center, Inc. v. Wisconsin Department of Revenue*, 84 Wis.2d 341, 267 N.W.2d 656 (1978).

[140] 464 A.2d 248 (Md. 1983). A third case, *Citizens and Southern Systems, Inc. v. South Carolina Tax Commission*, South Carolina Supreme Court Opinion No. 22024, reached the same decision.

[141] The analysis set out here is more fully developed in "Software and Sales Taxes: The Illusory Intangible," *B.U.L. Rev.* 63 (1983), p. 181.

[142] 287 Md. 178, 411 A.2d 439 (1980).

[143] Ibid. 287 Md. at 186, 411 A.2d at 443.

[144] Ibid. 287 Md. at 188, 411 A.2d at 444.

[145] See *Anthony Pools v. Sheehan*, 295 Md. 285, 455 A.2d 434 (1983); *Burton v. Artery Company*, 279 Md. 94, 367 A.2d 935 (1977); *Quotron* did not say that the dominant purpose of obtaining data made the subject of the contract intangible because information is intangible.

[146] 465 F.2d 615 (D.C. Cir. 1972).

[147] This form over substance argument was also adopted by the court in *Chittenden Trust Company v. King*, 465 A.2d 1100 (Vt. 1983).

[148] 465 A.2d 1100 (Vt. 1983).

APPENDIX A

Methodology

Several research methodologies were employed in the course of this study.

Review of Literature

A comprehensive review of the literature was completed to determine the extent of research previously undertaken. Literature on the financial accounting aspects of software accounting was found to be practically nonexistent. *FASB Statement No. 2*, "Accounting for Research and Development Costs,"[1] touches on the issue, as do *FASB Interpretation No. 6*, "Applicability of FASB Statement No. 2 to Computer Software,"[2] and *FASB Technical Bulletin 79-2*, "Computer Software Costs."[3] The Association of Data Processing Service Organizations also had a few relevant publications.[4] Only one article of any substance was in print at the time the present research was initiated.[5] Literature on the tax aspects of software was more readily available.[6] A number of court cases dealing with sales, use, property and investment tax credit have also been decided.

Interviews

Upon completion of the review of literature, a series of interviews were conducted with people who were knowledgeable in various aspects of software accounting. Telephone interviews were conducted with more than 20 individuals representing several facets of the software industry. Eighteen additional individuals representing seven software vendors and internal users were interviewed personally on company premises.

The Review Panel

Upon completion of the interviews, it became apparent that more empirical data needed to be gathered. A list of topics and specific questions was then written and sent to a review panel for comment using a modified version of the Delphi technique. Upon receiving panel member comments, a revised list of proposed questions was written and sent to panel members for further comment. This process was repeated several times until it was felt that further mailings to panel members would no longer be of significant value.

Panel members were selected in several ways. All members of the National Association of Accountants' (NAA) Management Accounting Practices (MAP) Committee were included, as were members of the NAA Subcommittee on MAP Statement Promulgation. Solicitation for members was also made in *Management Accounting*[7] and *Association Leader*,[8] NAA publications having a monthly circulation of 97,000 and 10,000 copies, respectively. Letters were also sent to 371 NAA chapter presidents requesting them to announce the search for panel members at their next chapter meeting. Some of the people who participated in the interviews also agreed to serve on the panel, as did members of the American Institute of Certified Public Accountants' (AICPA) Task Force on Accounting for the Development and Sale of Computer Software. The panel that reviewed the software vendor questionnaire was composed of 57 people. The internal user questionnaire was reviewed by 47 people.

The Sample

The sample for the vendor questionnaire was drawn from 30 known public companies and 368 other software vendors, some of which were public and some privately held. The latter group was selected randomly from *Data Sources* (Summer 1982) and the *1982 Data Decisions Software Vendor Directory*. All selected firms had annual revenues in excess of $5 million, although some earnings could have been derived from nonsoftware sources. The questionnaire was accompanied by a cover letter addressed to the chief financial officer. A self-addressed prepaid envelope was also enclosed. Eighty-eight usable responses were received for a response rate of 22.1 percent. A summary of findings is included in Chapter 3.

The sample for the internal user questionnaire was randomly drawn from the *Fortune 1000* and specialty lists. Four hundred fifty questionnaires, cover letters addressed to the controller, and prepaid envelopes were mailed. There were 216 usable responses, for a response rate of 48 percent. A summary of findings for this survey is in Chapter 5.

Computer Surveys

In addition to the mail questionnaire surveys and personal interviews that were conducted as part of the present study, a search of software vendor and user accounting policies was made using the NAARS data base.[9] A summary of the software cost and revenue recognition policies for more than 50 publicly traded companies in the software industry is included in Chapter 2.

A second survey using NAARS searched the financial statement footnotes of 4,197 companies for fiscal 1981-82 and 3,104 companies for fiscal 1982-83 for mention of software accounting policy. The software industry firms that were included in the other NAARS search were excluded. The summary in Chapter 4 includes only software user companies. One hundred twenty-five companies listed on NAARS had the word *software* listed in their accounting policy footnote. Some companies appeared twice, once for each fiscal year searched. Some firms were included in the software industry search, and so are excluded from this summary. Other firms mentioned software in a context that was not relevant for purposes of this study. Policies for the remaining firms were included in Chapter 4.[10]

Notes to Appendix A

[1] Financial Accounting Standards Board, *FASB Statement No. 2* (Stamford, Conn: 1974). Copies of the complete document are available from the Financial Accounting Standards Board, High Ridge Park, Stamford, Conn. 06905.

[2] Financial Accounting Standards Board, *FASB Statement No. 6* (Stamford, Conn. 1975).

[3] Financial Accounting Standards Board, *Technical Bulletin 79-2* (Stamford, Conn.: 1979).

[4] "Accounting Guidelines for the Computer Services Industry," *Exposure Draft*, April 1982; also, "Accounting Guidelines for the Computer Services Industry," survey conducted August 1982, published January 1983. Both published by the Association of Data Processing Service Organizations.

[5] Gary W. Burns and D. Scott Peterson, "Accounting for Computer Software," *The Journal of Accountancy*, April 1982, pp. 50-51, 53-54, 56, 58.

[6] See Michael J. Bayer, "*Citizens Financial Corporation* v. *Kosydar:* Data Processing and the Ohio Sales Tax Service Exemption," *Capital University Law Review*, 6 (1977), pp. 663-672; Robert P. Bigelow, "The computer and the Tax Collector," *Emory Law Journal* 30 (Spring 1981), pp. 357-93; John W. Bryant and Lance R. Mather, "Property Taxation of Computer Software," *New York Law Forum* 18 (Summer 1972), pp. 59-75; Matthew A. Case, "Sales and Use Tax of Computer Software—Is Software Tangible Personal Property?," *Wayne Law Review* 27 (Summer 1981), pp. 1503-36; Robert D. Crockett, "Software Taxation: A Critical Reevaluation of the Notion of Intangibility," *Brigham Young University Law Review*, no. 4, (1980), pp. 859-79; Data Processing Management Association, *Position Statement on Software Taxation*, Data Processing Management Association Position Statement, April 1982, p. 8; G. Davidson, "Collection of State Sales and Use Tax on Interstate Transfers of Computer Programs," *Jurimetrics Journal* 17 (Summer 1977), p. 286; Roy N. Freed, "A Legal Perspective on Sales Taxation of Software Programs," *Taxes*, September 1982, pp. 696-99; Karl K. Heinzman, "Computer Software: Should It Be Treated As Tangible Property For Ad Valorem Tax?," *The Journal of Taxation*, September 1972, pp. 184-86; Ronald Mangiacapra, "Computer Software—Availability of Investment Tax Credits," *The Tax Advisor*, December 1978, pp. 729-30; John G. Martin, "The Revolt Against the Property Tax on Software: An Unnecessary Conflict Growing Out of Unbundling," *Suffolk University Law Review*, Fall 1974, pp. 118-44; Harold S. Peckron, "Taxation of Computer Hardware and Software," *The Tax Executive*, October 1977, pp. 16, 59-77; Debra M. White and Michael T.

Vanecek, "Taxpayer Beware! The Current State of Computer Software Taxation," *Taxes*, May 1982, pp. 373-77.

[7]Robert W. McGee, "Accounting for Software—A Progress Report," *Management Accounting*, January 1983, pp. 38, 66.

[8]Robert W. McGee, "Software Accounting Is New MAP Project." *Association Leader*, January 1983, pp. 1-2.

[9]NAARS has financial statement data on more than 4,000 public companies and is available by subscription from the American Institute of Certified Public Accountants.

[10]Thanks go to Robert Kueppers of Deloitte Haskins and Sells in New York, who provided me with access to the NAARS data base.

APPENDIX B

Internal Revenue Service Pronouncements on Software

Rev. Rul. 71-177

Summary: For depreciation and investment credit purposes, the cost of a new computer includes software cost not separately stated and capitalized in accordance with the taxpayer's consistent practice.

Text: During 1968, a taxpayer purchased a new computer. The cost of the software provided with the computer was not separately stated. In accordance with his consistent practice, the taxpayer capitalized the entire cost of the computer, including the cost of the computer, including the cost of the software provided with it, and deducted depreciation thereon based upon a useful life in excess of four years.

Held, the cost of the computer, in the instant case, includes the cost of the software provided with it for purposes of the depreciation allowed under section 167 of the Internal Revenue Code of 1954 and the investment credit allowed under section 38 of the Code.

Rev. Rul. 71-248

Summary: The capitalization of software costs with respect to a new computer where such costs had previously been expensed is a change in method of accounting requiring the Commissioner's consent.

Text: Advice has been requested as to the proper treatment for Federal income tax purposes of certain software costs under the circumstances described below.

A corporation purchased a computer in 1965 which is still in use. Software costs incurred in connection with that computer have been expensed for both book and Federal income tax purposes.

In 1970, the corporation purchased a new computer which was installed in 1971. The installation of the new computer required the development by the corporation of an entirely new set of software for use with it. Software costs were incurred by the corporation in 1970 in connection with programming the new computer that the corporation desires to defer and amortize. Annual software costs in small amounts will continue to be incurred and deducted with respect to the old computer.

Specifically the question here relates to whether the deferral and amortization of software cost incurred in connection with the new computer method of accounting requiring the Commissioner's consent.

Section 3.01-1 of Revenue Procedure 69-21, C.B. 1969-2, 303, states that the costs of developing software by a taxpayer (whether or not the particular software is patented or copyrighted) in many respects so closely resemble the kind of research and experimental expenditures that fall within the purview of section 174 of the Internal Revenue Code of 1954 as to warrant accounting treatment similar to that accorded such costs under that section. Accordingly, it was stated that the Service would not disturb a taxpayer's treatment of costs incurred in developing software where all the costs properly attributable to the development of software by the taxpayer are consistently treated as current expenses and deducted in full in accordance with rules similar to those applicable under section 174(a) of the Code.

In addition, section 3.01-2 of Revenue Procedure 69-21 states that the Service would not disturb a taxpayer's treatment of costs incurred in its developing software where all the cost properly attributable to the development of software by the taxpayer are consistently treated as capital expenditures that are recoverable through deductions for ratable amortization, in accordance with rules similar to those provided by section 174 (b) of the Code and the regulations thereunder, over a period of five (5) years from the date of completion of such development or over a shorter period where the taxpayer clearly establishes that such costs have a useful life of less than five years.

Section 1.174-3 (a) of the Income Tax Regulations permits research and experimental expenditures to be treated on a project by project basis.

Revenue Ruling 68-144, C.B. 1968-1, 85, holds that where a taxpayer had elected to currently expense all research and experimental expenditures with the exception of those on particular projects to which the deferred expense method was elected, it cannot in a later year elect the deferred expense method on new projects unless permission is granted by the Commissioner.

Since as stated above, the costs of developing software closely resemble the kind of research and experimental expenditures that fall within the purview of section 174 of the Code, such software costs may be treated on a project by project basis. Thus, the corporation which has treated as current deductions the costs of software in connection with the old computer, may capitalize software costs with respect to the new computer only where permission is granted by the Commissioner.

An application for permission to change to a different method of treating software costs shall be in writing and shall be addressed to the Commissioner of Internal Revenue, Attention T:I, Washington, D.C. 20024. The application shall include the name and address of the taxpayer, shall be signed by the taxpayer (or his duly authorized representative) and shall be filed no later than the last day of the first taxable year for which the change in method is to apply. The application shall:

1. State the first year to which the requested change is to be applicable.
2. State whether the change is to apply to all software costs paid or incurred or only to expenditures attributable to a particular project.
3. Include such information as will identify the projects to which the change is applicable.
4. Indicate the number of months selected for amortization of the costs, if any, which are to be treated as deferred expenses.
5. State that, upon approval of the application, the taxpayer will make an accounting segregation on his books and records of software costs to which the change is to apply.
6. State the reasons for the change.

Rev. Proc. 69-21

Summary: Guidelines in connection with the examination of Federal income tax returns involving costs incurred to develop, purchase, or lease computer software.

Text: Section 1. Purpose

The purpose of this Revenue Procedure is to provide guidelines to be used in connection with the examination of Federal income tax returns involving the costs of computer software.

Section 2. Background

For the purpose of this Revenue Procedure, "computer software" includes all programs or routines used to cause a computer to perform a desired tax or set of tasks, and the documentation required to describe and maintain those programs. Computer programs of all classes, for example, operating systems, executive systems, monitors, compilers and translators, assembly routines, and utility programs as well as application programs are included. "Computer software" does not include procedures which are external to computer operations, such as instructions to transcription operators and external control procedures.

Section 3. Costs of Developing Software

.01 The costs of developing software (whether or not the particular software is patented or copyrighted) in many respects so closely resemble the kind of research and experimental expenditures that fall within the purview of section 174 of the Internal Revenue Code of 1954 as to warrant accounting treatment similar to that accorded such costs under that section. Accordingly, the Internal Revenue Service will not disturb a taxpayer's treatment of cost incurred in developing software, either for his own use or to be held by him for sale or lease to others, where:

1. All of the costs properly attributable to the development of software by the taxpayer are consistently treated as current expenses and deducted in full in accordance with rules similar to those applicable under section 174(*a*) of the Code; or

2. All of the costs properly attributable to the development of software by the taxpayer are consistently treated as capital expenditures that are recoverable through deductions of ratable amortization, in accordance with similar to those provided by section 174(*b*) of the Code and the regulations thereunder, over a period of five years from the date of completion of such development or over a shorter period where such costs are attributable to the development of software that the taxpayer clearly establishes has a useful life of less than five years.

Section 4. Costs of Purchased Software

.01 With respect to cost of purchased software, the Service will not disturb the taxpayer's treatment of such costs if the following practices are consistently followed:

1. Where such costs are included, without being separately stated, in the cost of the hardware (computer) and such costs are treated as a part of

the cost of the hardware that is capitalized and depreciated; or

2. Where such costs are separately stated, and the software is treated by the taxpayer as an intangible asset the cost of which is to be recovered by amortization deductions ratably over a period of five years or such shorter period as can be established by the taxpayer as appropriate in any particular case if the useful life of the software in his hand will be less than five years.

Section 5. Leased Software

Where a taxpayer leases software for use in his trade or business, the Service will not disturb a deduction allowable under the provisions of section 1.162-11 of the Income Tax Regulations, for rental.

Section 6. Application

.01 The costs of development of software in accordance with the above procedures will be treated as a method of accounting. Any change in the treatment of such costs is a change in method of accounting subject to the provisions of sections 446 and 481 of the Code and the regulations thereunder.

.02 For taxable years ending after October 27, 1969, the date of publication of this Revenue Procedure, the Service will not disturb the taxpayer's treatment of software costs that are handled in accordance with the practices described in this Revenue Procedure.

.03 For taxable years ending prior to the date of publication of this Revenue Procedure, the Service will not disturb the taxpayer's treatment of software costs except to the extent that such treatment is markedly inconsistent with the practices described in this Revenue Procedure. For the purpose of applying the preceding sentence, the absence of any formal election similar to that required by section 174 of the Code, or the amortization of capitalized software costs over a period other than the five-year period specified in section 174(b) of the Code, will not characterize the taxpayer's treatment of such costs as markedly inconsistent with the principles of this Revenue Procedure.

APPENDIX C

Sales and Use Tax Status of Software by State

Introduction

This tabular listing is designed to provide general information only regarding the tax status of computer programs. It is not to be construed as determinative of tax liability. Note that not all states have taken a formal position with respect to the taxability of programs. Footnotes to the table are at the end of the appendix.

This table is an updated version of a list prepared and copyrighted (1983) by Ronald J. Palenski, Associate General Counsel of ADAPSO, and is reprinted here by permission.

Sales and Use Tax Status of Computer Programs by State

State	Prewritten Programs	Custom Programs	Authority
Alabama	E[1]	E	Rule C28-001
Arizona	E	E	Rule 15-5-1853(c); Rule 15-5-1513(c)
Arkansas	T[1]	T	Informal Opinion (1979)
California	T[2]	E[2]	Cal. Rev. & Tax Code § 6010.9; Reg. 1502
Colorado	E[3]	E[3]	Special Regulation
Connecticut	T	T[4]	Conn. Gen. Stat. § 12-407(2); Bulletin #3
District of Columbia	E	E	District of Columbia v. Universal Computer Associates, Inc., 465 F.2d 615 (D.C. Circuit 1972)
Florida	E[3,5]	E	Rule 12A-1.32(4)
Georgia	T	T	Informal Opinion (1982)
Hawaii	T	T[6]	Information Opinion (1982)
Idaho	T	T	Regulation 12-2
Illinois	E[5]	E	86 Ill. Ad. Code § 130.1935
Indiana	E[5]	E	Rev. Information Bulletin #8
Iowa	T	T[7]	Rule 18.34
Kansas	T	T	K.S.A. 79-3603(s)
Kentucky	T	T	Informal Opinion (1982)

Louisiana	E	E	Art. 47:301(6)	
Maine	T	E	Informal Opinion (1982)	
Maryland	T	E	*Equitable Trust Co. v. Comptroller*, 464 A.2d 248 (Md. 1983)	
Massachusetts	T	T[7]	Reg. 64H.06	
Michigan	T	E	*Maccabees Mutual Life Insurance Co. v. State Dept. of Treasury*, 122 Mich. App. 660, 332 N.W. 2d 561 (1983)	
Minnesota	T[8]	E	Minn. Stat. § 297A.01(3)(a); Reg. 610	
Missouri	T	E	*James v. Tres Computer Systems, Inc.* 642 S.W. 2d 347 (Mo. 1982)	
Nebraska	E	E	Rev. Rul. 1-81-4	
Nevada	T	T	Informal Opinion (1981)	
New Jersey	E[3,5]	E[3]	N.J. Ad. Code 18:24-25.1	
New Mexico	T	T[6]	G.R. Reg. 3(K):2; G.R. Reg. 3(F):64	
New York	E[3,5]	E[3]	TSB 1978-(1)(S)	
North Carolina	T[9]	E	Informal Opinion (1982)	
North Dakota	E[3,5,10]	E[3,10]	Technical Memorandum	
Ohio	T	T[11]	Ohio Rev. Code § 5739.01	
Oklahoma	T	?[12]	Okla. Stat. tit. 68, § 1354(H)	
Pennsylvania	T	T	Reg. 163	
Rhode Island	T	T[7]	Reg. - Computers and Related Systems	
South Carolina	T	T	Reg. 117-174.262; *Citizens and Southern Systems, Inc. v. Tax Commission*, Opinion No. 22024 (January 10, 1984)	
South Dakota	T	T[4]	Reg. 64:06:02:79; Reg. 64:06:02:80	
Tennessee	T	T	Tenn. Code § 67-3002(b)	
Texas	E[13]	E	Tex. Admin. Code tit. 34, § 3.308	
Utah	T	E	Informal Opinion (1982)	
Vermont	T	E	*Chittenden Trust Co. v. King*, 465 A.2d 1100 (Vt. 1983)	
Virginia	T	T[7]	Informal Opinion (1981)	
Washington	T	E[14]	ETB 515.04.155	
West Virginia	T	T	Informal Opinion (1982)	
Wisconsin	T	T[7]	Proposed Rule 11.71	
Wyoming	T	T	Wyo. Stat. § 39-6-404(a)(xiii)	

Notes to Appendix C

[1] E = Exempt; T = Taxed.

[2] Assembly Bill 2932, enacted September 22, 1982, exempted custom computer programs generally (except basic operating programs) whether in human or machine-readable form. Also exempted were modifications to prewritten programs, designed specifically for a single user.

[3] Software is generally considered to be intangible so long as there is: (*a*) vendor analysis of user requirements or (*b*) modification of software to fit a particular hardware/software configuration.

[4] Custom programs transferred in human-readable form are taxed as services rather than as tangible personal property.

[5] Computer game cartridges and similar mass-distribution programs do not qualify for exemption.

[6] Custom programs are taxed as services rather than as tangible personal property.

[7] Custom programs are taxable if sold, leased, or licensed in machine-readable form; custom programs are exempt if sold, leased, or licensed in human-readable form, such as program instructions listed on coding sheets.

[8] Effective July 1, 1983, only programs will require vendor modifications to meet the specific requirements of the customer will be regarded as intangible property exempt from sales and use taxation; otherwise, programs sold off-the-shelf will be regarded as tangible and subject to tax.

[9] Effective August 1, 1983, all prewritten programs are subject to sales and use taxation while custom programs are not. A custom program is one prepared to the special order of the customer and includes specially prepared modifications to prewritten programs. A program is regarded as custom if there is: vendor analysis of user requirements or modification of software to fit a particular hardware/software configuration.

[10] In order to preserve the program exemption, charges for tangible media (for example, tapes and cards) must be separately billed, and the tax for such applied.

[11] Effective July 1, 1983, a variety of computer services, including the "designing, selling, lessing, modifying, or debugging of specialized or customized computer programs," became subject to sales and use taxation in Ohio.

[12] Because of the peculiar wording of the Oklahoma statute (referencing both "software" and "prewritten programs"), it is unclear whether custom programs are taxable or exempt. In particular cases, please consult local counsel.

[13] This exemption extends even to home computer game cartridges.

[14] Note that services such as custom programming are subject to the Business and Occupation Tax.

Bibliography

"A New Weapon Against Japan: R&D Partnerships." *Business Week*, August 8, 1983, p.42.

Accardo, S. F. "Computer Software." In *Corporate Finance Research*, Shearson/American Express, November 9, 1982.

"Accounting for Software Costs." *Issues Paper* prepared by the Task Force on Accounting for the Development and Sale of Computer Software, Accounting Standards Division, American Institute of Certified Public Accountants, January 1984.

Adams, Naomi. "Programming Computer Software Into Financial Statements." *Going Concerns*, Queens College Accounting Honor Society, October 19, 1983, p. 4.

Alex. Brown & Sons. "Industry Accounting Concerns." *Computer Services Monthly*, August 1982.

American Institute of Certified Public Accountants. *Statements of the Accounting Principles Board No. 4*. "Basic Concepts and Accounting Principles Underlying Financial Statements of Business Enterprises." New York: AICPA, October 1970.

———. *Industry Accounting Guide*. "Accounting for Motion Picture Films." New York: AICPA, 1973.

———. "Securities and Exchange Commission." *AICPA Washington Report*, August 8, 1983, p. 1.

———. *Statement of Position 76-1*. "Accounting Practices in the Record and Music Industry." New York: AICPA, 1976.

———. *Statement of Position 79-4*. "Accounting for Motion Picture Films." New York: AICPA, 1979.

Arcady, Alex T. "Accounting for Computer Software Costs." Speech at the Software Accounting Conference, sponsored by the National Association of Accountants, Washington, D.C., September 9, 1983.

Arthur Andersen & Company. "Moratorium on Capitalizing Cost of Internally Developed Software." *Accounting News Briefs*, September 1983, pp. 2-3.

———. "Research and Development." *Washington Tax Letter*, September 23, 1983, p. 3.

Arthur Young & Company. "Proposed Regulations on Credit for Increasing Research Activity-Internal Revenue Code Sections 44F and 174." Letter addressed to Commissioner of Internal Revenue dated March 25, 1983.

_____. "Proposed Treasury Regulation Section 1.174-2(a) (3) and (4)." Letter addressed to Commissioner of Internal Revenue dated March 16, 1983.

Association of Data Processing Service Organizations. "Accounting Guidelines for the Computer Services Industry." *Exposure Draft.* April 1982.

_____. "Accounting Guidelines for the Computer Services Industry." Survey conducted August 1982. Published January 1983.

Balthasar, Hans Ulrich; Roberto A. A. Boschi; and Michael M. Menke. "Calling the Shots in R&D." *Harvard Business Review,* May/June 1978, pp. 151-60.

Barres, John. "Tracking the Accounting and Taxation Methods of the Computer Software Industry." MBA thesis, New York University, 1984.

Barry, R. J.; S. Goldstein; and T. M. Brehmer. "Proposed Regs. on the Credit for Research and Experimental Expenditures: An Analysis." *The Journal of Taxation,* August 1983, pp. 76-83.

Battaglia, Jack M., and Donald L. Herskovitz. "Organizing a Computer Software Research and Development Program for Top Tax Advantage." *The Journal of Taxation,* February 1983, pp. 92-96.

Beresford, Dennis R., and Robert D. Neary. "Financial Reporting Briefs." *Financial* Executive, July 1983, pp. 8-9.

Bierman, Harold, and Roland E. Dukes. "Accounting for Research and Development Costs." *The Journal of Accountancy,* April 1975, pp. 48-55.

Bisgay, Louis. "Management Accounting Practices." *Management Accounting,* June 1983, pp. 8, 73.

_____. "Management Accounting Practices." *Management Accounting,* July 1983, pp. 8, 23.

_____. "Management Accounting Practices." *Management Accounting,* August 1983, pp. 10, 34.

_____. "Management Accounting Practices." *Management Accounting,* November 1983, pp. 8, 80.

Blakeney, Susan. "Tax Act May Include Cuts for Software." *Computerworld,* June 28, 1982, pp. 1, 8.

Burns, Gary W., and D. Scott Peterson. "Accounting for Computer Software." *The Journal of Accountancy,* April 1982, pp. 50-51, 53-54, 56, 58.

Computer and Business Equipment Manufacturers Association. "Computer Industry Leaders Declare IRS Violating Congressional Intent on Software Regulations." *Industry News,* April 7, 1983.

"Computer-Software Developers Find Hope in the Research-Credit Dispute." *The Wall Street Journal,* April 27, 1983, p. 1.

"Computer Tax Rules Assailed." *New York Times,* April 25, 1983, p. D2.

"Comserv Restates Its Results to Show Wider Loss in 1st Half." *The Wall Street Journal,* September 26, 1983, p. 13.

Craig-Hallum, Inc. "Comserv Corporation." *Notes from Research,* August 25, 1982.

Damsky, Gerald. "Integration of the Section 44F Research Tax Credit into the Research Investment Venture." *Taxes,* February 1983, pp. 127-36.

Datapro Research Corporation. "A Review of Software Cost Estimation Methods." In *EDP Solutions.* Delran, N.J.. Datapro, 1978, p. E40-350-601-615.

_____. "Estimating Software Development Costs." In *EDP Solutions.* Delran, N.J.: Datapro, 1976, p. E40-350-501-507.

_____. "Hidden Software Development Costs." In *EDP Solutions*. Delran, N.J.: Datapro, 1976, p. E40-350-701-710.

Deloitte, Haskins & Sells. *Survey of Accounting Policies: Public Companies in the Computer Software Industry*. New York: Deloitte, Haskins & Sells, February 1982.

Deutsch, Dennis S. *Protect Yourself: The Guide to Understanding and Negotiating Contracts for Business Computers and Software*. New York: John Wiley & Sons, 1984.

DiBernardo, S. James. "The Taxation of High Technology." *Taxes*, December 1983, pp. 813-28.

Duryea, R. Terry. "Accounting for Computer Software." Speech at the Software Accounting Conference, sponsored by the National Association of Accountants, Washington, D.C., September 9, 1983.

E. F. Hutton. "Comserv Corp.: Forbes Article Reaction Rating Increased From 3-1 to 2-1." Wire No. 18. January 10, 1982.

Ernst & Whinney. "SEC Freezes Software Capitalization Policies." *Financial Reporting Briefs*, August 1983, p. 2.

"Expenses, Shmexpenses." *Forbes*, May 23, 1983, p. 13.

"*FASB Interpretation No. 6*—Applicability of *FASB Statement No. 2* to Computer Software." *The Journal of Accountancy*, April 1975, pp. 65-6.

Feinschreiber, Robert. "Defining Research for Purposes of the Research Credit." *The Tax Executive*, January 1983, pp. 159-66.

Financial Accounting Standards Board. *FASB Interpretation No. 6*. "Applicability of *FASB Statement No. 2* to Computer Software. Stamford, Conn.: 1975.

_____. *Status Report No 85*. "*FASB Statement No. 2* and *Interpretation No. 6*." April 9, 1979.

_____. *Statement of Financial Accounting Concepts No. 2*. "Qualitative Characteristics of Accounting Information." Stamford, Conn., 1980.

_____. *Statement of Financial Accounting Standards No. 2*. "Accounting for Research and Development Costs." Stamford, Conn., 1974.

_____. *Statement of Financial Accounting Standards No. 48*. "Revenue Recognition When Right of Return Exists." Stamford, Conn., 1981.

_____. *Statement of Financial Accounting Standards No. 50*. "Financial Reporting in the Record and Music Industry." Stamford, Conn., 1981.

_____. *Statement of Financial Accounting Standards No. 53*. "Financial Reporting by Producers and Distributors of Motion Picture Films." Stamford, Conn., 1981.

_____. *Statement of Financial Accounting Standards No. 68*. "Research and Development Arrangements." Stamford, Conn., 1982.

_____. *Technical Bulletin 79-2*. "Computer Software Costs." Stamford, Conn., 1979.

Fingleton, Eamonn. "Capital Offense." *Forbes*, January 17, 1983, pp. 100-101.

_____. "U.S. Laws Hit Hi-Tech." *Accountancy Age*, April 21, 1983, p. 21.

Frank, Werner L. *The New Software Economics*. Silver Spring, MD: United States Professional Development Institute, Inc., 1979.

Gannon, John J., and David Parkinson. "Software Development Costs Should be Expensed." *Management Accounting*, November 1983. pp. 37-9.

Hawkins, David F. "Technology Accounting Traps." *Accounting Bulletin 1*. Drexel Burnham Lambert, Inc., March 1983.

"High-Tech Companies Team Up in the R&D Race." *Business Week*, August 15, 1983, pp. 94-95.

Horwitz, Bertrand, and Richard Kolodny. "Has the FASB Hurt Small High-Technology Companies?" *Harvard Business Review*, May–June 1980, pp. 44, 48, 52.

_____. "The Economic Effects of Involuntary Uniformity in the Financial Reporting of R&D Expenditures." *Journal of Accounting Research*, Supplement, 1980, pp. 38–107.

_____. "The FASB, the SEC and R&D." *The Bell Journal of Economics*, Spring 1981, pp. 249–62.

_____. "The Impact of Rule Making on R&D Investments of Small High-Technology Firms." *Journal of Accounting, Auditing and Finance*, Winter 1981, pp. 102–13.

Hudson, Richard L. "SEC Halts Spread of Accounting Method That Increases Profit of Software Firms." *The Wall Street Journal*, April 15, 1983, p. 10.

_____. "SEC May Curb Accounting Rule for Software." *The Wall Street Journal*, April 8, 1983, p. 52.

Ijiri, Yuji. *The Foundation of Accounting Measurement*. Houston: Scholars Book Co., 1978.

"The IRS Should Reconsider." *Business Week*, May 2, 1983, p. 144.

"The IRS Takes a Hard Line on Software." *Business Week*, May 2, 1983, p. 31.

"IRS Proposals on R&D Are Inadequate High Tech Incentive." *Entrepreneur*, August 1983, p. 32.

Jaenicke, Henry R. *Survey of Present Practices in Recognizing Revenues, Expenses, Gains, and Losses*. Stamford, Conn.: FASB, 1981.

Ketz, J. E., and J. Walker. "Software Packages: Should a Firm Make or Buy Them?" *Cost and Management*, July–August 1978, pp. 43–6.

Kudla, Ronald J., and Thomas H. McInish. "A New Tool for R&D Project Evaluation." *Industrial Management*, November/December 1980, pp. 5–7.

Langs, Edward F. "Vendor's View of Computer Contracts." In *Purchasing and Leasing Computers and Software*. New York: Practising Law Institute, 1979, pp. 59–68.

Lindhorst, W. Mike. "Scheduled Maintenance of Applications Software." *Datamation*, August 1973, pp. 64–7.

Littrell, Earl K. "Death of an Asset—The R&D Blood Bath." *Management Accounting*, January 1981, p. 63.

Machinery and Allied Products Institute. "Computer Software: SEC Proposes Accounting and Disclosure Rules for Internal Costs of Developing Computer Software for Sale or Lease to Others." *Executive Letter*, May 2, 1983.

_____. "Research and Experimentation: MAPI Presentation to Treasury Department and Internal Revenue Service Urges Liberalization of Research Tax Credit Proposals With Respect to Independent Research and Development of Government Contractors, Computer Software Development, and Research in Other Contexts." *Executive Letter*, May 2, 1983.

Mangiacapra, Ronald. "Computer Software—Availability of Investment Tax Credits." *The Tax Advisor*, December 1978, pp. 729–30.

McGee, Robert W. *Accounting for Software Costs*. New York: National Association of Accountants, 1984.

_____. "Accounting for Software Costs." *Seton Hall University Faculty Working Paper Series*. 1984.

_____. "Accounting for Software Costs—A Summary of Findings." *Management Accounting*, February 1984, pp. 38–9.

_____. "Accounting for Software—A Progress Report." *Management Accounting*, January 1983, p. 38, 66.

———. "Accounting for Software Costs Study Is Under Way." *Association Leader*, October 1983, pp. 1, 9.

———. "Software Taxation: A New NAA Research Study." *Management Accounting*, March 1984, pp. 70–71, 77.

———. "Software Taxation." *Seton Hall University Faculty Working Paper Series*. 1984.

———. *Fundamentals of Accounting and Finance*. Englewood Cliffs, N.J.: Prentice-Hall, 1983.

———. *The Effects of Software Accounting Policies on Bank Lending Decisions and Stock Price*. New York: National Association of Accountants, 1984.

———. "The Effects of Software Accounting Policies on Bank Lending Decisions and Stock Price." *Seton Hall University Faculty Working Paper Series*, 1984.

———. "Software Accounting is New MAP Project." *Association Leader*, January 1984, pp. 1–2.

———. "NAA Software Study is Complete." *Association Leader*, January 1984, pp. 1, 10.

———. *Software Taxation*. New York: National Association of Accountants, 1984.

———. "Computer Software and the Research Credit," *Computer Law Journal*, Fall 1984.

———. "Sales, Use and Property Taxation of Computer Software," *Hamline University Law Review*, Fall 1984.

———. "Financial and Tax Accounting for Computer Software," *Northern Kentucky Law Review*, Fall 1984.

———. "Software Accounting, Bank Lending Decisions and Stock Price," *Management Accounting*, July 1984, pp. 20, 23.

———. "Computer Software and the Investment Tax Credit," *Computer Law Journal*, Fall 1984.

———. "Financial Accounting for Computer Software," *Occasional Paper*, Deakin University, Victorian, Australia, 1984.

McGee, Robert W., and John Gibbs. *Let Accounting Help You Manage*. Englewood Cliffs, N.J.: Prentice-Hall, 1981.

———. *Financial Decision-Making in Business*. Englewood Cliffs, N.J.: Prentice-Hall, 1980.

Myers, Edith D. "What is Software?" *Datamation*, March 1979, p. 74.

Neal, Roger. "Caution for Lotus-Eaters." *Forbes*, September 26, 1983, pp. 52, 54.

Pakin, Sandra. "Software Info: Evaluate User Documentation Before You Buy the Software." *Infosystems*, October 1980, pp. 91–96.

Paulsen, Neil E. "Software Development Costs Should Be Capitalized." *Management Accounting*, November 1983, pp. 40–42.

Practising Law Institute. *Computer Law 1982: Acquiring Computer Goods and Services*. New York, 1982.

———. *Purchasing and Leasing Computers and Software*. New York, 1979.

Price Waterhouse. "A Moratorium Can Be More Than a Freeze." *Accounting Events and Trends*, June–July 1983, p. 2.

———. "From SEC." *Accounting Events and Trends*, August, 1983, p. 5.

———. "Software Development Costs." *Accounting Events and Trends*, May 1983, p. 3.

———. "Software Development Costs—Asset or Expense." *Accounting Events and Trends*, March–April 1983, p. 2.

Pridemore, Charles. "Software: Should Development Costs Be Expensed or Capitalized?" *Management Accounting*, November 1983, p. 33–36.

Rev. Proc. 69-21, 1969-2 CB 303.

Rev. Rul. 71-177, 1971-1 CB 5.

Rev. Rul. 71-248, 1971-1 CB 55.

Riopel, Robert J. "Accounting for Software Development Costs." Speech at the Software Accounting Conference, sponsored by the National Association of Accountants, Washington, D.C., September 9, 1983.

———. "Software Development: Asset—or Liability?" *Financial Executive*, December 1983, pp. 22–24, 26.

Schmitz, Homer H. "There's More Than One Consideration for the Accounting Treatment of Purchased Software." *Hospital Financial Management*, August 1975, p. 21–24.

Securities and Exchange Commission. "Accounting for Costs of Internally Developing Computer Software for Sale or Lease to Others." 17 CFR Parts 210 and 239; Release Nos. 33-6476; 34-20061; FR-12; File No. S7-968, August 8, 1983. Published in the *Federal Register*, vol. 48, no. 157, August 12, 1983, 36566-36571.

Seed, Allen H., III. "Management Accounting for Software Development," *Corporate Accounting*, Summer 1984, pp. 14–19.

Seidler, Lee J. "SEC Finalizes Moratorium on Capitalizing Software Costs." *Accounting Issues*, Bear, Sterns & Co., September 27, 1983, pp. 5–7.

Seneker, Harold, and Jayne A. Pearl. "Software to Go." June 20, 1983, pp. 93–95, 98–100, 102.

"Software Development Costs: An Accounting and Tax Problem." *Accounting News*, Summer 1983, pp. 16–17.

"Software Maintenance: Expensive Problem." *The Economist*, December 18, 1982, p. 92.

Srinivasan, Cadambi A., and Paul E. Dascher. "Manage Each Step For Quality Software." *Hospital Financial Management*, May 1979, pp. 18–24.

"Suppliers Battling Software Costs." *Electronic News*, September 12, 1983, pp. 17, 22.

"Task Force of AcSEC Studies Computer Software Accounting." *The Journal of Accountancy*, June 1983, p. 9.

Treasury Department. "Credit for Increasing Research Activity." 26 CFR Part 1. Published in the *Federal Register*, vol. 48, no. 15, January 21, 1983, 2790–2800.

United States General Accounting Office. *Illustrative Accounting Procedures for Federal Agencies: Guidelines for Automatic Data Processing Costs*. Federal Government Accounting Pamphlet Number 4, GAO, 1978.

Upton, Molly. "FASB Clarifies October Ruling Defining Software Costs as R&D." *Computerworld*, March 19, 1975, p. 9:6.

Wasserman, Michael G. "Section 174 and Computer Software Development." *Taxes*, August 1983, pp. 506–512.

Zech, K. P. "Selecting the Right Software." *The Journal of Accountancy*, June 1982, pp. 112–118.

Index

A
Ability to raise capital, 57, 59, 88-104
Accounting Principles Board, 4
AICPA, 12, 18
Amortization, 13-17
  user policies (footnotes), 65-77
  user questionnaire, 78
  vendor policies (footnotes), 18-52
  vendor questionnaire, 53, 61
Arthur Andersen & Co., 62
Arthur Young & Co., 62
Association of Data Processing Service Organizations (ADAPSO), 12, 158
Author's views, 12-17

B-C
Bibliography, 161-66
Bruns, W. J., Jr., 89
Capitalization, 11-14, 53-64, 78-87
Classification of software, 16, 54-55, 62, 81, 84
Coding costs, 13-14, 56
Collapsible corporation, 3

D
Deloitte Haskins & Sells, 18, 64
Design costs, 13-14
Diagram, 14
Disclosure, 16, 54-55, 81
Dopuch and Ronen, 89
Dyckman, T. R., 89

E
Effects
  on growth, 59
  on interest rate, 58-59, 94, 104
  on net income, 60
El-Arabi, A. A., 89
El-Maksy, M. M., 89
Ernst & Whinney, 62

F
Falk and Ophir, 89
FASB Concepts Statement No. 3, 11
FASB Interpretation No. 6, 7-8, 16, 149
FASB Statement No. 2, 4-7, 16, 149
FASB Statement No. 50, 9-10
FASB Statement No. 53, 10
FASB Technical Bulletin No. 79-2, 8, 149
Feasibility, 13-14
Financial accounting, 1, 4
Financial Accounting Standards Board (FASB), 4, 9

I
Individual-software-forecast-computation method of amortization, 15-16
Internal Revenue Service, 2, 3, 106, 153-57
International Business Machines Corporation (IBM), 1, 2, 11 105
Interviews, 13
Investment tax credit, 3, 17, 61, 83

J-K

Jain, T. N., 89
Jensen, R. E., 88
Knowledge rationale, 109
Kueppers, Robert, 18, 64

L-M

Leased software, 81
Litigation, 62
Methodology, 149-52
Mlynarczyk, F. A., 89
Mode of transmission test, 110
Motion picture films, 10, 14, 110-13

N

NAARs, 18, 64
National Bureau of Standards, 107
National Commission on New Technological Uses of Copyrighted Works, 9

O-P

O'Donnell, J. L., 88
Palenski, Ronald J., 158
Period-table-computation method of amortization, 14-15
Personal service rationale, 109
Price Waterhouse, 62
Property taxation, 3, 17, 105-32

R

Record and music industry, 9-10, 110
Relative value test, 109
Replevin, 3
Research credit, 61, 83, 86
Research and development arrangements, 10-11, 60-61
Rev. Proc. 69-21, 155-57
Rev. Rul. 71-177, 153
Rev. Rul, 71-248, 153-55
Revenue recognition policies of software vendors, 18-52

S

Sales and use tax, 3, 17, 105-32
  status of software by state, 158-60
Sales of information
  artwork, 117-18
  credit information, 116
  mailing lists, 116-17
  stock exchange data, 114-16
Securities and Exchange Commission, 12, 83
Service bureau tax cases, 119-22
Service costs, 13-14
Software accounting policy and bank lending decisions, 88-104
Software definitions, 3, 106-9
Software user accounting policies, 64-77
Software user survey summary, 78-87
Software vendor accounting policies, 18-52
Software vendor survey summary, 53-63
State taxation, 3, 105-32
Staubus, George J., 88
Summers, Edward L., 88
Support costs, 13-14

T

Tangibility, 3, 109-11
Testing costs, 13-14
Touche Ross & Co., 62

U-W

Unbundling, 1, 105
Uniform Commercial Code, 3, 118-19
U.S. Bureau of Standards, 107
Warranty, 56

HF 5681 .C57 M37 1985 c.1
McGee, ~~DISCARD~~
Accounting for software

Saginaw Valley State College Library
DATE DUE

DEC 14 1996			

DEMCO 38-297